Kugels from our Tanta's

Kim's Favorite Kugel

My Favorite Kugel

By Nan Saretsky

Kugels from our Tanta's

By Nan Marcel Saretsky

Copyright © 2021
Nan Marcel Sartsky
All rights reserved.

Printed in the U.S.A.

ISBN 978-1-09836-293-5

Dedicated to the memory of Kim Holly Saretsky Endlich

On November 9th, 2008, my younger sister, Kim, passed away leaving behind a son Hudson, who was not even two years old, a husband David, our dad, William, brother Roy, myself, and my children. She was predeceased by our mother, Harriet. She was a cherished mother, beloved wife, devoted daughter, loving sister, and the best aunt anyone could ask for. She also left behind other family and friends who loved her so much.

Kim would make a kugel recipe from one of our aunts and I would make one from a different aunt. We used to joke that one day we would put together a cookbook and title it: Kugels from our Tanta's (Yiddish for aunts). I have decided to do this cookbook and dedicate it to her memory. It has been a labor of love. Kim's memory will always live on in the hearts and souls of all that loved her. Her son, Hudson, is now 14 years old and we tell him stories of his Mom. She would have loved so much to see her son grow up and see his wonderful accomplishments. She should be here for this. My four children have grown up, married, and had children of their own. Heather (Michael) Shoshi and Avi Jacobsohn, Jennifer (Morgan) Ethan and Davis Chemij, Benjamin (Molly) Luna and Daisy, Myriah (Nick) Gavin and Lilah Kimberly Monical (who was named for Kim, keep her memory alive).

To my sister Kim, Kimmie, Kimala and Kimbo, we all love you and miss you so much. Your memory will always live on in the hearts of the many people who loved you so much!

What is a kugel?

A kugel is a baked pudding or casserole, and while commonly associated and made with noodles, they are also made with potatoes, rice, breads, fruit, vegetables, matza, farfel, and sometimes a combination of interesting ingredients. The staple ingredients that make a kugel are a starch base, eggs and fat. Throughout this book you will see many versions of kugels. Kugels are served warm or cold, as a side dish or as dessert.

Kugels date back to the 12h century, first made in Germany from bread and flour. It spread throughout Eastern Europe and the Jewish women added rendered fat which is a testament to random poverty they suffered. During the 17th century, sugar became popular and kugels evolved from only savory to also sweet. Kugel is a Yiddish term coming from the German word for ball or sphere. They used to be made in round pans. Today kugels are usually made in rectangular or square pans.

The kugels in this book come from family, friends, and people around the world who wanted to share their family favorite kugels in this cookbook. I appreciate all of them for allowing me to publish their treasured recipes. Many contributors talked about the memories they have while they are cooking them. Noodle Kugels are the most popular.

Throughout this book you will see the Yiddish word for noodle written in a variety of ways. Yiddish originated during the 9th century, used by Jews in central and eastern Europe. Yiddish is a combination of Hebrew, Aramaic, German, Slavic languages and the Romance languages. Kugels are traditional to our Jewish heritage and became a favorite comfort food. Our ancestors would steam kugels in a pot.

Two of my grandchildren happily sang this Yiddish song that they learned in preschool.

Yiddish	English
BULBES	POTATOES
Zuntik-bulbes	Sunday-potatoes
Montik-bulbes	Monday-potatoes
Dinstik un mitvokh-bulbes	Tuesday and Wednesday-potatoes
Donershtik un fraytik-bulbes	Thursday and Friday-potatoes
Ober Shabes in a novine	But on Shabbos something special
!A bulbe kigele	A potato kugel!
Un zuntik vayter-bulbes	And Sunday-and so on

Table of Contents

Chapter 1: Kugels from the Family of Kim and Me

1. Aunt Karolyn's Luckshen Kugel
2. Aunt Sylvia's Luckshen Kugel
3. My Daughter Heather's Apple Kugel
4. My Daughter Heather's Challah Kugel
5. My Daughter Heather's Passover Apple Crumb Kugel
6. Our Aunt Rozy's Luckshen Kugel
7. Our Aunt Emma's Luckshen Kugel
8. Our Cousin Pam's Potato Latke Kugel
9. Our Cousin Lin's Sweet Noodle Kugel
10. Our Cousin Lin's Parve Luckshen Kugel
11. Our Cousin Ellen's Vegetable Kugel
12. Our Cousin Yvonne's Potato Kugel
13. Our Cousin Yvonne's Lokshen Kugel
14. Our Cousin Betty's Potato Kugel

Chapter 2: Noodle, Luckshen, Lokshen, Lukcheon, Luchen, Lockshen, Luxel, Lichen

1. Upside-Down Plum Noodle Kugel
2. Suzanne's Holiday Noodle Kugel
3. Velvet Noodle Pudding
4. Shelly's Noodle Kugel
5. Lokshen Kugel from Rose
6. Noodle Pudding from Shawna
7. Golden Milk Noodle Muffin Tin Kugel
8. Jody's Noodle Kugel
9. Eva's Pineapple-Raisin Dairy Noodle Kugel
10. Noodle Pudding from Betty
11. Peach Noodle Kugel (Parve)
12. Jerusalem Kugel
13. Gail's Lokshen Kugel
14. Grandma Pearl's Noodle Pudding
15. Milchige (Dairy) Lukcheon Kugel

16. Lukshen Kugel from Susan
17. Two Tone Kugel
18. IRC's Noodle Kugel
19. Savory Noodle Kugel
20. Gwyn Nanus' Noodle Kugel
21. Ellen's Noodle Kugel
22. Grandma Selma's Noodle Kugel
23. Gail's Noodle Kugel
24. Mom's Noodle Kugel
25. Beth's Noodle Kugel
26. Noodle Kugel Cupcakes
27. Pineapple Noodle Kugel from Chris
28. Noodle Kugel from Howard
29. Karen's Luchen Kugel
30. Sweet Noodle Kugel from Diane
31. Sweet Noodle Kugel from Suzanne
32. Sweet-Crunchy Kugel
33. Coconut Noodle Kugel
34. Noodle Kugel with Candied Pecans
35. Noodle Pudding from Renee
36. Pumpkin Noodle Kugel
37. Fran's Delicious Noodle Kugel
38. Mom's Famous Noodle Pudding
39. Francyn's Noodle Kugel
40. Jill's Sweet Kugel
41. Rhonda's Family Cheese Kugel
42. Naomi's Easy Yerushalayim Kugel
43. Apple Honey Raisin Noodle Kugel
44. Donna's Spinach Noodle Kugel
45. Grandma K's Kugel
46. Estee's Luckshen Kugel
47. Aunt Mickey's Kugel
48. Elayne's Noodle Kugel
49. Flora's Noodle Kugel
50. Aunt Debbie's Kugel
51. Grammie Shirley's Prize Winning Noodle Kugel

52. Noodle Pudding from Sarna's Great Grandmother
53. Leslie's Noodle Kugel
54. Noodle Kugel with Pineapples
55. One-Step Noodle Kugel
56. Hodge Podge Kugel
57. Barbara's Noodle Pudding
58. Artichoke and Brie Kugel Bites
59. Bubbie Florence's Kugel
60. Family Kugel Recipe from Tracy
61. Noodle Kugel with Peas and Parmesan
62. Lokshen Kugel from Lynda
63. Noodle Kugel from Nancy
64. Yummy Kugel
65. Bea's Noodle Kugel
66. Kate's Noodle Kugel
67. Skinny Noodle Kugel
68. Tasty Noodle Pudding
69. Fabulous Noodle Kugel
70. Especially on Shavuot Noodle Kugel
71. Laura Sherman's Sweet Lockshen Kugel
72. Noodle Kugel from Mt. Kisco, N.Y.
73. Applesauce Noodle Kugel
74. Noodle Kugel from Sharona
75. Kimberly's Luckshen Kugel
76. Estelle's Spinach Noodle Kugel
77. Noodle Kugel from Marion
78. Dorothy's Noodle and Cheese Kugel
79. Luxel Kugel from Donna
80. Noodle Kugel from Ryan
81. Sweet Kugel from Rhonda
82. Hope's Noodle Kugel
83. Bubi's Noodle Kugel
84. Sticky Bun Kugel
85. Eileen's Noodle Kugel
86. Lemon Ricotta Kugel with Dried Fruit Medley
87. Noodle Kugel from the Beth El Congregation

88. Freddie's Kugel
89. Kugel from Carla's Great Grandma
90. Grandma Goldie's Noodle Pudding
91. Lichen Kugel from Linda
92. Dessert Kugel
93. Cheesecake Kugel
94. Nikki's Pineapple Noodle Kugel
95. Gluten Free Noodle Kugel
96. Aunt Florrie's Sweet Noodle Kugel
97. Valerie's Noodle Kugel
98. Debbie's Noodle Kugel

Chapter 3: Vegetable and Fruit Kugels

1. Diane's Carrot Kugel
2. Laura's Apple Streusel Noodle Kugel
3. Zucchini and Mushroom Kugel
4. Grandma Selma's Apple Kugel
5. Judith's Onion Kugel
6. Beautiful Tri-Layered Vegetable Kugel
7. Sweet Spaghetti Squash Kugel
8. Dorit's Squash Kugel
9. Carrot Ring Kugel
10. Squash Kugel from Shayna
11. Butternut Squash Kugel from Diane
12. Cabbage Kugel from our Ancestors
13. Diane's Onion Kugel
14. The Best Apple Kugel
15. Spaghetti Squash Kugel
16. Ima Audrey's Squash Kugel
17. Malky's Apple Kugel
18. Ilene's Vegetable Kugel
19. Apricot and Apple Streusel Kugel
20. Rikki's Onion Kugel
21. Eggplant Kugel
22. Laura's Mom's Kugel

23. Family Favorite Carrot Kugel
24. Broccoli Kugel from Fran
25. Five Vegetable Kugel
26. Walnut and Broccoli Kugel
27. Nana Elma's Kugel
28. Corn Kugel
29. Onion Kugel

Chapter 4: Potato, Rice, Bread and Vegan Kugels

1. Broccoli-Potato Kugel
2. Bernice's Potato Kugel
3. An Easy Potato Kugel
4. Annie's Rice Kugel
5. Challah Vegetable Kugel from Diane
6. Ima's Sweet Potato Kugel with Pineapple
7. Potato and Leek Kugel
8. Flour Kugel
9. Ruth's Vegan Sweet Potato Kugel
10. Delicious Potato Kugel
11. Challah Kugel! Yum
12. Carole's Vegan Potato Kugel
13. Ronda's Rice Kugel
14. Fresh Hot Potato Kugel
15. Bread Kugel
16. Tasty Rice Kugel
17. Sharon's Vegan Potato Kugel
18. Georgette's Family Potato Kugel
19. The BEST Potato Kugel Ever
20. Sweet Potato Kugel
21. Pan Fried Potato Kugel
22. Daniel's Potato Kugel
23. Marlene's Vegan Noodle Kugel
24. Leya's Potato Kugel
25. Vegan Sweet Potato Kugel

Chapter 5: Passover Kugels

1. Apple Matza Kugel
2. Anita's Passover Potato Kugel
3. Passover Apple Kugel
4. Myrna's Matzo Farfel Kugel
5. Spinach and Broccoli Kugel
6. Ilene's Sweet Kugel
7. Mom's Matzo Kugel
8. Passover Pineapple Kugel
9. Renana's Passover Vegetable Kugel
10. Ima Audrey's Mushroom Pesach Kugel
11. Pesach Carrot Kugel
12. Apple Farfel Kugel
13. Ima's Pesach Banana Kugel
14. Matzo Kugel from Ryann
15. Linda's Matzoh Kugel
16. Melanie's Zucchini and Potato Kugel
17. Aunt Helen's Matzoh Kugel
18. Zucchini Kugel
19. Matzo and Mushroom Kugel
20. Joan's Passover Pineapple Kugel
21. Mini Meat and Matza Kugel
22. Passover Vegetable Kugel

Chapter 1: Kugels from the Family of Kim and Me

1. Aunt Karolyn's Luckshen Kugel
Kim's Favorite from Our Aunt Karolyn Sklar, currently residing in Sarasota, Fl.

Ingredients
8 oz. package of broad noodles
6 eggs
½ pt. sour cream
¾ cup sugar
½ t. salt
1 t. vanilla
1 small can of evaporated milk
2 T. butter or margarine
raisins
cinnamon and sugar

Preparation
Preheat oven to 350 degrees. Cook noodles. Pour noodles over raisins and "plump" raisins. Cream together eggs, sour cream and sugar. In a separate small bowl, beat evaporated milk, salt and vanilla with a fork. Fold all ingredients with noodles and raisins. Put butter in an 8x8 or a 9x9 baking dish. Put dish into the oven until butter bubbles. Add noodle mixture and sprinkle with cinnamon and sugar. Bake for ½ hour, or until "set."

This freezes well. Be sure to thaw completely before reheating.
Enjoy!

2. Aunt Sylvia's Luckshen Kugel
My favorite from our Aunt Sylvia Rosler, deceased, born in Russia and last resided in Hallandale, Fl.

Ingredients
10 eggs
1 ½ c. sugar
½ t. salt
2 T. vanilla

6 oz. cream cheese
1 lb. cottage cheese
1 pt. sour cream
3 sticks butter or margarine, melted
1 lb. fine noodles
graham cracker crumbs for the topping

Preparation
Cook the noodles according to the package directions. Beat eggs, sugar, salt and vanilla together. Blend cheeses and sour cream. Add the melted butter or margarine to the egg mixture. Place the mixture together with the noodles into a 13x9 glass baking dish. put the graham cracker crumbs on top. Bake at 350 degrees for one hour.
Enjoy!

3. My Daughter Heather's Apple Kugel
Submitted by my daughter, Heather Sabra Jacobsohn, currently residing in Potomac, Md. She makes this sweet kugel for Rosh Hashana.

Ingredients
4 eggs, beaten
1 cup sugar
2 teaspoons cinnamon
½ cup oil
1 cup flour
1 teaspoon baking powder
6 tart apples, peeled and sliced
½ cup raisins, optional

Preparation
Combine eggs, sugar, cinnamon, and oil. Stir in flour and baking powder. Fold in sliced apples and raisins. Pour into a well-greased 9x13 inch pan and bake in a 350° preheated oven for 45–50 minutes.

4. My Daughter Heather's Challah Kugel
Submitted by my Daughter, Heather Jacobsohn, currently residing in Potomac, Md.

Ingredients
12 ounce challah, pulled into bite size chunks
1 ½ cups water
1 ½ cups rice/soy milk
4 eggs beaten
½ cup sugar
1 teaspoon vanilla
2 tart green apples
2 tablespoons melted margarine

Preparation
Soak challah in liquid. Add the other ingredients and pour into a well-greased pan. Bake for one hour at 375°.

5. My Daughter Heather's Passover Apple Crumb Kugel
Submitted by my daughter, Heather Jacobsohn, currently residing in Potomac, Md.

Ingredients for filling
3 apples, peeled and thinly sliced
1 t. lemon juice
2 T. sugar

Ingredients for crumbs
½ cups crushed ladyfingers
½ cup ground almonds
1 cup sugar
1 t. baking powder, optional but recommended
1 egg
½ cup oil

Preparation
Preheat oven to 350 degrees. Lightly grease a 9x13 baking pan.

To prepare filling
Place thinly sliced apples in a bowl, toss with lemon juice immediately to prevent browning. Add sugar and set aside.

To prepare crumbs
Mix together the ladyfinger crumbs, ground almonds, sugar and baking powder in a large bowl. Add the egg and oil and stir with your fingers until coarse crumbs are formed.

Place a little less than half of the crumbs on the bottom of the prepared baking pan. Spread the apple filling evenly over the crumbs. Pour remaining crumbs over the apples, spread in an even layer to ensure that all apples are covered.

Bake at 350 for about 40 minutes, until golden brown on top.

Note from Heather: The kugel was very thin when made as directed above. Next time she will make it (and there definitely will be a next time) she will bake it in a 10 inch round pan to make a slightly higher kugel.

Enjoy!

6. Our Aunt Rozy's Luckshen Kugel
Submitted by our Aunt Roslyn Braun, born in the Bronx, NY and currently residing in Wharton, N.J.

Ingredients
1 lb. wide egg noodles
1 cup sugar
6 beaten eggs
16 oz. large curd cottage cheese
8 oz. cottage cheese
1 pt. sour cream
1 stick melted butter
½ cup mixed cinnamon/sugar

Preparation
Grease a 9x13 pan and preheat oven to 325 degrees (glass) other pans to 350
Cook noodles "al dente" and cool. Beat eggs and sugar for 2 minutes. Add cream cheese and beat until fairly smooth (there will be a few lumps). Add cottage cheese, sour cream and melted butter. Add noodles and mix to incorporate. Pour into pan and sprinkle with cinnamon and sugar.

Optional items can be added to mixture before baking: raisins, slivered almonds, fruit salad or crushed pineapple, drained.

Bake for 1 hour and 5 minutes.

7. Our Aunt Emma's Luckshen Kugel
Submitted by our Cousin Donna Rothstein
This is our Aunt Emma's Luckshen Kugel. Aunt Emma is now deceased, born in the Bronx, NY and last resided in Yonkers, N.Y.

Ingredients
1 pkg. of broad egg noodles
6 eggs
16 oz. cottage cheese
16 oz. sour cream
1 cup sugar
1 T. lemon juice
3 T. butter
black pepper

Preparation
Boil noodles drain and place in an 11x7 baking dish. Melt the butter in a small pot on low heat. In a large bowl, mix the eggs. Add cottage cheese, sour cream, sugar, a little bit of black pepper and lemon juice. Mix all of the ingredients together. Pour the mixture over noodles and stir everything together. Next, pour the melted butter on top of the noodles and stir it again.

Bake at 350 degrees for 45-60 minutes. Check it with a fork, if it comes out clean, it is good to go.

8. Our Cousin Pam's Potato Latke Kugel
Submitted by our Cousin Pam Ronner currently residing in Stamford, Ct.

Ingredients
5 lb. bag of Idaho potatoes
2 lbs. onions
12 eggs
2 cups of matzo meal, unsalted
salt and pepper to taste
oil
aluminum large sized rectangular pan

Preparation
Preheat oven to 350 degrees. Pour one inch of oil into the pan and heat it in the oven. Peel the potatoes and make sure that they are clean and dry. Cut both the potatoes and the onions into squares. Using a blender (not a food processor), put in two eggs and a few pieces of onion and blend until onion is liquid. While the blender is still going, drop pieces of potato in until you reach the top of the blender. Pour out in a very large bowl and repeat until all of the potatoes and onions and eggs are gone, stirring the batter well. Add matzo meal until the batter has thickened to a cake batter or thicker consistency. Add salt and pepper to taste.

Carefully (if you can get a helper, do so) pull the heated oil from the oven and immediately pour batter in. It should sizzle and may splatter so be careful. The batter will rise before it falls so don't fill the pan to the top or oil will spill over. Put back in oven until the kugel is golden brown, crisp on sides, hard in center, for about an hour or more. It will continue to cook after you remove it from the oven so it's best you let it cool a bit before cutting.

9. Our Cousin Lin's Sweet Noodle Kugel
Submitted by our Cousin David Rubin, from his late wife, Aline Rubin, last residing in Codrington, Ontario, Canada.

Ingredients
12 oz. noodles
3 eggs
½ c. sugar
½ pint sour cream

12 oz. cottage cheese
½ c. milk
½ c. butter
raisins
corn flakes
brown sugar

Preparation
Cook noodles. Beat eggs until foamy. Add sugar gradually and continue beating. Add sour cream, cottage cheese, milk, melted butter and raisins. Put in a greased 9x13 oven proof casserole. Sprinkle corn flake crumbs mixed with brown sugar over kugel. Drizzle more melted butter on top. Cover with foil. Bake at 350 degrees for 1 hour.

10. Our Cousin Lin's Parve Luckshen Kugel
Submitted by our Cousin David Rubin from his late wife, Aline Rubin last residing in Codrington, Ontario, Canada

Ingredients
12 oz. pkg. noodles, broad or fine
4 eggs, beaten
Salt and pepper, to taste
2 tbsp. oil

Preparation
Cook noodles according to the package directions. Drain and rinse well. In a large bowl, combine noodles, eggs and seasoning. Mix well. Heat oil in a casserole in a 375 degree oven. Add hot oil to noodle mixture and mix well. Bake for one hour, until lightly browned. Makes 8 servings.

Note: Add 2 tbsp. sugar, 1 tsp. cinnamon and ¼ cup raisins to noodles for a sweet kugel.

11. Our Cousin Ellen's Vegetable Kugel
Submitted by our Cousin, Ellen Ettinger, currently residing in Beacon Bay, South Africa

Ingredients
4 oz. margarine or a ½ cup of oil
8 T matzo meal
1t baking powder
3 T potato flour
8T kiddush wine
1 lb grated carrots
2 oz raisins and additional optional chopped dried dates
3 oz brown sugar
1 t cinnamon
orange or apple juice plus one rind of either
2 beaten egg
½ t salt

Preparation
Cream margarine and sugar and add the matzo meal. Dissolve the potato flour in wine. Mix all of the ingredients together and bake in an ungreased dish for about one hour at 350F or 180 C.

12. Our Cousin Yvonne's Potato Kugel
Submitted by our Cousin Yvonne Hurwitz, currently residing in White Rock, British Columbia, Canada.

Ingredients
6 potatoes, pared and grated
2 T. flour
2 eggs
salt and pepper
½ t. cinnamon
½ t. grated onion
3 T. oil
paprika for top

Preparation
Boil potatoes and drain well. Pare or grate. Blend in flour, eggs and all of the seasonings. Mix well. Heat oil in a casserole dish, add batter plus a little oil on top. Sprinkle top with paprika and bake in a 400° oven for one hour.

13. Our Cousin Yvonne's Lokshen Kugel
Submitted by our Cousin Yvonne Hurwitz, currently residing in White Rock, British Columbia, Canada.

Ingredients
12 oz. pkg. noodles, broad or fine
4 eggs, beaten
2 T. chicken fat or oil
salt and pepper
2 T. sugar (optional)
½ c. raisins (optional)

Preparation
Boil noodles according to the package directions. Drain well, in a large bowl, add beaten eggs, seasonings and mix well. Transfer to a casserole dish and add chicken fat or oil. Bake for one hour at 350°.

14. Our Cousin Betty's Potato Kugel
Submitted Bynum cousin Betty Hurwitz, currently residing in Montreal, Quebec, Canada.

Ingredients
6 peeled potatoes, mashed
1 egg
3 onions
1 c. crushed cornflakes

Preparation
Fry onions in oil. Add the mashed potatoes and mix well. Add the egg and crushed cornflakes. Put in a casserole dish and bake for 40 minutes at 350 degrees. Take kugel out of the oven and top with paprika. Broil for 15 minutes until the top is crispy.

Chapter 2: Noodle, Luckshen, Lokshen, Lukcheon, Luchen, Lockshen, Luxel, Lichen Kugels

1. Upside-Down Plum Noodle Kugel
Submitted by Lisa Paul Young, currently residing in Newtown, Pa.

Ingredients
8 ounces egg noodles
¾ cup cottage cheese
½ cup sour cream
¼ cup melted butter
⅓ cup sugar
3 eggs
¼ t. vanilla extract
½ t. salt
1 red plum, sliced

Preparation
Preheat the oven to 350 degrees. Boil the egg noodles according to the package directions- al dente. In a large bowl, mix the cottage cheese, sour cream, butter, sugar, eggs, vanilla extract and salt. Mix in the cooked egg noodles until well combined. Grease a bundt pan. Slice a plum and place each slice at the bottom of the pan. Add the noodle mixture and flatten with a spatula. Bake for 50 minutes until crispy on top.
Using the spatula, loosen the edges. When the bundt pan is cool, place a plate on top and flip it over. Jiggle the pan until the kugel comes free and falls onto the plate. Sprinkle with cinnamon.

2. Suzanne's Holiday Noodle Kugel
Submitted by Suzy Shalom, currently residing in Bicester, Oxfordshire, England

Ingredients
1 stick margarine
8 oz. softened cream cheese
4 eggs, lightly beaten
7 t. sugar
2 t. vanilla
½ t. salt

lemon juice, to taste
8 oz. wide egg noodles, cooked and drained
cinnamon and sugar for topping

Preparation
Preheat oven to 350 degrees. Blend margarine and cream cheese together. Mix in sour cream, eggs, sugar, vanilla and salt, one at a time. Blend well. Stir in lemon juice and noodles. Pour mixture into an 11x13 inch greased pan. Sprinkle the top with sugar and cinnamon and bake for one hour.

If you are health conscious, Suzy has made this recipe using low fat ingredients and cut eggs in half and used an egg substitute for half.

3. Velvet Noodle Pudding
Submitted by Diane Dubey, currently residing in Lincolnwood, Il.

Ingredients
1/4 pound butter, melted
1 8-ounce package cream cheese
4 eggs
1/2 cup sugar
1 cup whole milk
1 teaspoon vanilla extract
8 ounces semi-broad noodles (cooked, drained and rinsed)

Topping
1 cup crushed corn flakes
1/2 teaspoon cinnamon
2 T sugar
2 T butter, melted

Preparation
Preheat oven to 350 degrees F. In a food processor or electric mixer, blend butter, cream cheese and eggs. Add sugar, milk and vanilla. Blend well. Transfer to a large bowl and add the cooked noodles. Blend. Pour into a greased oven-to-table 8 1/2 x 11-inch serving dish. Combine topping ingredients and spread over noodles. Bake for 1 hour.

4. Shelly's Noodle Kugel
Submitted by Judi Rosenberg
This recipe was given to her by her friend, Shelly, in 1980 and has been making it ever since.

Ingredients
½ lb. fine noodles
8 eggs
1 lb. butter or margarine
1 c. sugar
2 t. vanilla
1 pt. sour cream
½ lb. cream cheese

Preparation
Grease a large aluminum pan. Cook noodles and drain in hot water. Put them on the bottom of the pan. Mix remaining ingredients until "smooth." Pour over noodles (don't stir).

For the topping
2 oz. butter
2 c. crushed sugared cereal flakes
2 ½ T. sugar and cinnamon

Melt butter and combine with the other ingredients in a bowl. Spread on top of kugel. Bake at 350 degrees for one hour and ten minutes.

5. Lokshen Kugel from Rose
Submitted by Rose Linden

Ingredients
Butter (for the dish)
Salt, to taste
1 pound medium or wide egg noodles
1 pint (2 cups) sour cream
1 cup golden raisins
1/2 cup (1 stick) unsalted butter, cut up

1 pound (2 cups) small curd cottage cheese
1 package (7.5 ounces) farmer cheese
1 cup sugar
2 teaspoons vanilla
8 eggs, beaten to mix
1 jar (12 ounces) apricot preserves
1 teaspoon ground cinnamon mixed with 2 tablespoons sugar (for sprinkling)

Preparation
Set oven to 350 degrees. Butter a 9-by-13-inch baking dish. Bring a large pot of salted water to a boil. Add the noodles and cook, stirring occasionally, for eight minutes or until they are tender but still have some bite (they should be slightly underdone because they'll cook more later). In a bowl, combine the sour cream and raisins; set aside for 10 minutes. Drain the noodles into a colander and return them to the pot. Add the butter and stir well. Stir in the cottage cheese, farmer cheese, sugar, vanilla, a large pinch of salt, eggs, and sour cream mixture. Pour half of the noodle mixture into the baking dish. Add a spoonful of apricot preserves in here and there. Top with the remaining noodle mixture. Sprinkle with cinnamon-sugar. Bake the pudding for 1 to 1 1/4th hours or until the mixture is set. Let it settle for 5 minutes before cutting into squares.

6. Noodle Pudding from Shawna
Submitted by Shawna Dyer currently residing in Simi Valley, Ca.

Ingredients
16 oz. wide egg noodles
5 large eggs
½ c. butter melted plus 2 T. melted butter and set aside
16 oz. full fat, large curd cottage cheese
16 oz. sour
8 oz. whipped cream cheese
2 t. vanilla extract
¾ c. sugar
½ t. salt
1 T. cinnamon sugar
cornflake crumbs

Preparation
Preheat oven to 350°. Grease a 9x13 baking dish. In a large pot, boil noodles until al dente. In a large bowl, whisk eggs, sugar, butter, salt and vanilla until well combined and sugar and salt are dissolved. Add cottage cheese, sour cream and cream cheese. Mix until well combined. Drain noodles. Combine noodles and mixture until fully coated. Spoon into pan. Cover top with a layer of cornflake crumbs. Pour 2 T. of butter to coat cornflakes. Sprinkle cinnamon on top. Bake uncovered for about 25 minutes (or less if starting to burn). Cover with foil and bake for 35 more minutes. Remove from oven and let sit for 5 to 10 minutes.

7. Golden Milk Noodle Muffin Tin Kugel
Submitted by Emilia Aronowitz

Ingredients
16 oz. medium egg noodles
4T. unsalted melted butter
16 ounces full-fat small curd cottage cheese
16 ounces sour cream
4 eggs, beaten
¼ C. granulated sugar
¼ C. light brown sugar
2 t. vanilla extract
1 ½ T. golden milk spice mix

Toppings
1 C. crushed corn flakes
1 t. golden milk spice mix
¼ C. sugar
2T. unsalted melted butter

Preparation
Heat oven to 350 degrees. Spray two nonstick muffin tins with cooking spray. Cook the noodles in salted boiling water to al dente. Drain and rinse with cold water. In a large bowl, toss the noodles with the melted butter. In a smaller bowl, mix the cottage cheese, sour cream, eggs, sugar, vanilla and golden milk spice mix. Pour over the buttered noodles and stir well. Fill the muffin cups to the top with the noodle mixture.

In a separate bowl, mix the corn flakes, sugar and spice mix. Toss with the melted butter and sprinkle the mixture on top of the noodle mixture. Bake for about 30 minutes until the top is crisp and the knife in the middle comes out clean. Let stand in the muffin tins for five minutes.

8. Jody's Noodle Kugel
Submitted by Jody Schwartz

Ingredients
1 lb. noodles cooked
2 cups boiled milk
1 cup sugar
1 stick butter
12 ounces cream cheese
4 eggs
1 t. vanilla
¼ cup sugar
¼ cup corn flake crumbs
1 t. cinnamon
¼ stick butter

Preparation
Preheat oven to 350 degrees. Cook noodles and drain. Boil milk on the stove. Mix milk, sugar, butter and cheese. Stir until melted. Mix into cooked and drained egg noodles. Stir well. Put into a buttered 9x13 pan. Mix the sugar, corn flake crumbs and cinnamon and sprinkle it on top. Dot with the ¼ stick butter. Bake for one hour.

9. Eva's Pineapple-Raisin Dairy Noodle Kugel
Submitted by Eva Tolub born in Bistrita, Transylvania, and currently residing in Mundelein, Il.

Ingredients
8oz. wide noodles, cooked and drained
8 oz. crushed pineapple, drained
8 oz. sour cream
1 cup white raisins
12 oz. cottage cheese

2 tsp. vanilla
2 eggs, slightly beaten
½ chopped walnuts
⅓ cup sugar
2 Tbsp. breadcrumbs
2 Tbsp. melted butter or vegetable oil
cinnamon

Preparation
In a large bowl, combine all ingredients, except pineapple, raisins, nuts and cinnamon. Mix well. Stir in drained pineapple, raisins and nuts and turn into a greased 2-to-3-quart baking dish. Sprinkle with cinnamon. Bake in a preheated 350-degree oven for about an hour, or until the top is nice and golden brown. Enjoy!

10. Noodle Pudding from Betty
Submitted by Beth Neshek Bobel of Wadsworth, Il.
Original Recipe from her friend, Betty Rothkopf of Albany, NY

Ingredients
3 eggs, separated
½ cup butter, melted
4 T white sugar
2 cups cottage cheese
1 cup sour cream
8 ounces cooked egg noodles
½ cup corn flakes, crushed
Additional butter to coat corn flakes

Preparation
Beat egg yolks. Add butter and white sugar. Fold in cottage, sour cream and noodles. Beat egg whites until stiffly beaten. Gently fold into noodle mixture. Place in buttered casserole dish. Top with butter and crushed corn flake crumbs.

Bake at 375 degrees for 45-60 minutes. Serves 8.

11. Peach Noodle Kugel (Parve)
Submitted by Karen Scott
This recipe is from her Aunt Gail Weber

Ingredients
8 ounces wide egg noodles
2 ¾ cup sugar
1 stick margarine, melted
1 lb. canned sliced peaches, drained
Cinnamon

Preparation
Boil noodles according to the package directions. Drain. Grease baking pan. Beat eggs, and add sugar, margarine and peaches. Place noodles in baking pan and egg mixture. Stir together. Sprinkle with cinnamon. Bake uncovered at 350 degrees for 45 minutes.

12. Jerusalem Kugel
Submitted by Diane Dubey, currently residing in Lincolnwood, Il.

Ingredients
2 (12-ounce) packages thin egg noodles
2/3 cup plus 5 T vegetable oil
4 eggs
3 cups sugar
2 T freshly ground black pepper
1 T kosher salt

Preparation
In a large pot of salted boiling water, cook the noodles according to package directions; drain well, toss with 1 tablespoon vegetable oil to prevent sticking, return to the pot, and reserve. In a medium saucepan combine the 2/3 cup oil with the sugar and cook over medium-low heat, stirring occasionally, making sure to watch for any signs of burning. This will not be like a regular caramel; parts will turn very dark brown, and it is likely that around the edges the sugar will take a while to dissolve. Most likely, the sugar and the oil will never fully unify. Put the caramel into the noodles and stir. Parts of the caramel harden immediately. Turn the flame

onto medium-low and warm the noodles, stirring, until the caramel dissolves, about 10-12 minutes. Remove from heat and cool to room temperature.

Preheat the oven to 375°F. Stir in the eggs, pepper and salt. In a 5 or 6-quart stockpot, heat the remaining 4 tablespoons of oil until very hot but not smoking. Add the egg-noodle mixture; do not stir, and let it cook on the stovetop, noting how the edges begin to darken, for 7-8 minutes.

Transfer to the oven and bake until the top is slightly hardened, for about 1 hour. Cool for 30 minutes, invert onto a serving platter, and either serve immediately or allow to cool completely. If you wait, the outer shell of the kugel will be chewy-crunchy.

13. Gail's Lokshen Kugel
Submitted by Gail Margolis Alpern, currently residing in Weston, Fl.

Ingredients for Filling
¼ lb. butter, melted
6 eggs
½ c. sugar
2t. vanilla
8 oz. container whipped cream cheese
1-pint sour cream
16 oz. box wide egg noodles, cooked

Topping
1 ½ c. crushed cornflakes
¼ lb. butter, melted
½ c. sugar

Preparation
Combine butter, eggs, sugar, and vanilla in a blender or food processor until well mixed. Add sour cream. Blend. Mix noodles with sour cream mixture. Pour into a 2-quart ovenproof casserole. Combine topping ingredients. Sprinkle over noodles. Cover. Freeze kugel. Bake while frozen. After kugel is frozen, bake covered at 400° for 1 ¾ -2 hours.

14. Grandma Pearl's Noodle Pudding
Submitted by Karen Scott
Karen loves thinking about her Grandma Pearl when making this.

Ingredients
4 eggs
½ lb. cottage cheese
½ c. sour cream
1 ½ -2 c. milk
1 t. vanilla
½ c. sugar
½ lb. noodles
2-3 small boxes of raisins

Preparation
Put all this together and refrigerate overnight. The next day, top with crushed corn flake crumbs plus ¼ t. cinnamon and sugar. Dab butter on top. Bake at 350 degrees for one hour and enjoy.

15. Milchige (Dairy) Lukcheon Kugel
Submitted by Marlene Snell from Harrisburg, Pa.
Marlene has happy memories of making this with her Mom who died in 1971

Ingredients
12-16 oz. extra wide egg noodles
6-8 Tbsp. butter, melted; extra butter to grease pan
1 can evaporated milk
1 milk-can of water
2 large eggs, beaten
1 tsp. cinnamon
1/2 tsp. vanilla extract
1/2-3/4 cup sugar
1 large apple, peeled, cored, and chopped
1/2-3/4 cup golden raisins, optional
1/2 cup cottage cheese, optional

Preparation
Set oven to 350-degree F. Grease a 13x9" glass pan. Cook the egg noodles according to package directions. Drain and set aside. Stir together butter, milk, water, eggs, cinnamon, and vanilla. Stir in sugar, then apple, raisins, and cottage cheese if using. Put noodles into a pan. Pour milk mixture over noodles, pressing raisins into milk mixture, making sure that all noodles are wet. Cover with foil and bake for about 40 minutes. Take off foil and bake about 20 minutes more. Don't let the top burn. It will be fairly solid but will "set" further as it cools. Serve warm or cold. Serve plain or topped with sour cream or canned pie filling (blueberry or cherry).

16. Lukshen Kugel from Susan
Submitted by Susan Oki, currently residing in Armonk, NY

Ingredients
1 lb. wide noodles
6 eggs
¼ c. sugar
1 lb. cottage cheese
½ lb. cream cheese
½ c. milk
1 pt. sour cream or yogurt
½ lb. butter, melted
1 c. white raisins, optional
1 t. vanilla

Preparation
Preheat oven to 350 degrees. Butter a 9x13 inch baking dish. Boil noodles in salted water. When cooked, drain and rinse under cold water and drain again. Beat eggs with sugar. Mash cream cheese with milk. Pour noodles in a bowl and add all of the other ingredients. Blend well and pour mixture into the baking dish.

Add topping as follows:
8 oz. cornflakes
¼ lb. butter, melted
1 c. brown sugar

Crumble the cornflakes with your hands; add brown sugar and melted butter, mixing thoroughly with your hands. Spread mixture over pudding. Bake for about 40 minutes.

17. Two Tone Kugel
Submitted by Diane Dubey

<u>Ingredients</u>
Yerushalayim Kugel Layer
1-1/4 cups sugar
1/2 cup oil
1 (10 oz) bag fine noodles, cooked
4 eggs
1 tsp salt
3/4 tsp black pepper

Sweet Lokshen Kugel Layer
1 (10 oz) bag fine noodles, cooked
1-1/4 cup sugar
1/3 cup oil
4 eggs
1 T vanilla sugar

Crumb Topping
2 1/2 cups crispy rice cereal
1/2 cup brown sugar
3 T oil

<u>Preparation</u>
For Yerushalim Kugel layer:
Preheat oven to 350, grease 2 medium loaf pans, set aside. Caramelize the sugar and oil in a saucepan over medium heat. Cook for about 30 minutes, stirring continually until caramel colored and liquid. Add cooked noodles to caramelized sugar, mix together and cool. Add eggs, salt, black pepper. Mix well, Divide yerushalmi kugel evenly into the 2 loaf pans.

For Sweet Lokshen Kugel layer:
Mix sugar, oil, eggs and vanilla sugar in bowl, add cooked noodles and mix well, pour over yerushalmi kugel layer

For crumbs:
Mix rice krispies cereal, brown sugar and oil in a bowl. Sprinkle over kugel.

Bake at 350 for 1 hour uncovered.

18. IRC's Noodle Kugel
Submitted by Connie Mencis

Ingredients
1 lb. medium wide egg noodles
¾ lb. creamed cottage cheese
1 ½ c. sour cream
1 T. vanilla
1 c. sugar
8 eggs
1 c. raisins-light or dark
¼ lb. butter, melted
1 can fruit cocktail (15 oz.)

For topping
1 c. sugar
1 t. cinnamon
⅔ c. crushed cornflakes

Preparation
Cook noodles until almost tender. Drain and add all of the other ingredients (except topping). Mix well. Turn into a 9x13 baking pan. Put on topping mixture. Bake at 350 degrees.

19. Savory Noodle Kugel
Submitted by Madi Greenberg

Ingredients
16 oz. egg noodles
4 eggs
Chopped chicken
Chopped sautéed onion
Sliced carrots
Sliced celery
1 can of cream of chicken soup
A few pinches of thyme
Chopped basil
Salt and pepper to taste
Breadcrumbs for topping

Preparation
Mix all of the ingredients together. Top with breadcrumbs. Bake covered at 350° for one hour. Uncover and bake for 10 minutes more at 400°.

20. Gwyn Nanus' Noodle Kugel
Submitted by Jen Marzouk from Chicago, Il.

Ingredients
1 lb. medium noodles
6 eggs
½ c. sugar
2 T. orange juice
2 T. vanilla
½ c. applesauce
1 stick margarine
1 can apple pie filling
Raisins

For the topping:
1 c. brown sugar

½ stick margarine
1 c. graham cracker crumbs

Preparation
Mix topping ingredients and set aside. Cream margarine and sugar. Add other ingredients and pour into baking dish. Bake at 350° for 30 minutes. Pour on the toppings and bake for an additional 15 minutes.

21. Ellen's Noodle Kugel
Submitted by Jen Marzouk from Chicago, Il.

Ingredients
1 pound medium flat noodles
1 quart buttermilk
5 eggs, beaten
¼ pound margarine, melted in pan
½ cup sugar
4 tablespoons applesauce
Cornflake crumbs

Preparation
Cook the noodles. Fold buttermilk into noodles. Refrigerate overnight. Add other ingredients. Pour into a 9x13 baking pan. Top with cornflake crumbs. Bake for one hour at 400°.

22. Grandma Selma's Noodle Kugel
Submitted by Jen Marzouk from Chicago, Il.

Ingredients
¾ stick butter + more
4 lbs. Jonathan or Granny Smith apples
2+2 T. flour
¾ c. brown sugar
¾ c. sugar

For the dough:
2 large eggs

1 eggshell of water (both halves)
1 ¾ cups flour
pinch of salt

Preparation
Combine eggs and water, then salt and flour until easy to handle. Refrigerate until ready. Melt butter in a shatterproof glass dish. Spread and pour off excess and save.

For the filling, peel and core apples and cut into chunks. If watery: dry. Mix apples with both sugars and 2 T. flour. Mix well with hands. Refrigerate while rolling dough. Roll out dough until large enough to cover the top, bottom, and sides. Smear with butter and sprinkle with 2 T. of flour. Put dough in pan. Put apples in pan. Lap dough over. Punch so irregular. Brush with butter. Bake at 350° for 1 hour. Brush with butter again. Cover with foil and bake for another 15 minutes.

23. Gail's Noodle Kugel
Submitted by Gail Siegel

Ingredients
1 pkg. noodles, fine or medium
4 eggs, beaten
¾ cup sweetener, to taste- sugar or artificial
½ cup margarine
Cinnamon to taste
Raisins
Chopped peaches (or any fruit)

Preparation
Cook noodles according to package directions. Mix all together. Bake at 350 degrees for 45 minutes until golden brown.

24. Mom's Noodle Kugel
Submitted by Lisa Sanetra, currently residing in Queens, NY

Ingredients
3/4th pound wide noodles
3 Tablespoons butter (cut into pieces)
1/4th pound bar cream cheese (cut into pieces)
3 eggs slightly beaten
1 cup cottage cheese
1 cup sour cream
1/2 cup sugar
1 teaspoon salt
1/2 teaspoon cinnamon

Preparation
Serves 6-8. Preheat oven to 350 degrees. Butter your pan. An 8x8 or 9x9 inch pan should be good for this recipe. Cook noodles according to package directions and drain. Place butter and cream cheese in a large bowl and add the hot noodles. Mix until the butter is melted, and the cream cheese is no longer in chunks. Add eggs, cottage cheese, sour cream, sugar, salt and cinnamon. Mix well. Spread evenly in the pan. Bake until cooked through and golden on top, approximately 35-45 minutes.

25. Beth's Noodle Kugel
Submitted by Beth Schwartz Rokuskie from Warminster, Pa.

Ingredients
1 stick butter
8 oz. cream cheese
2 cups sour cream
4 eggs, beaten
7 T. sugar
2 t. vanilla
½ t. Salt
Package of wide egg noodles

Preparation
Preheat oven to 350 degrees. Mix first 7 ingredients into the mixer. Cook the package of noodles as directed, and then add noodles to the mixture. Mix together with a large spoon. Pour into a buttered casserole or lasagna dish. Bake for one hour at 350, then sprinkle cinnamon and sugar mixture on top.

26. Noodle Kugel Cupcakes
Submitted by Diane Dubey

Ingredients
5 eggs
1/2 cup sugar
One teaspoon vanilla
1/2 cup oil
1 cup apple sauce
1 cup diced pineapple fresh or canned
1/2 teaspoon cinnamon
3/4 cup of pecans
3/4 cup dried cranberries
1 pack cooked wide noodles

Preparation
Mix all the ingredients by the order off the list. Grease the cupcake pan. Bake on 350 for 25 minutes.

27. Pineapple Noodle Kugel from Chris
Submitted by Chris

Ingredients
1 pkg. wide egg noodles
1 container pineapple cottage cheese or plain cottage cheese
3 cups milk
6 eggs
2/3 cup sugar
1 can pineapple chunks, drained

Preparation
In your blender, blend milk, eggs, cottage cheese and sugar (you may have to blend in batches). Set aside. Cook noodles al dente. Drain. Place in a buttered 9x13 pan. Arrange in an even layer. Add cheese mixture. Top with pineapple chunks, stirring in lightly. You can sprinkle cinnamon on top, if you like. Bake 350 degrees for about 45 minutes till well set and slightly browned on top.

28. Noodle Kugel from Howard
Submitted by Howie Rubin from South Bend, In.
This is now his favorite kugel

Ingredients
1/2 pound wide egg noodles (sometimes I add a little extra like an oz or two)
1/2 stick unsalted butter, melted (I used 3/4th)
1 pound cottage cheese
2 cup sour cream
1/2 cup sugar
6 eggs (used 7 jumbos)
1 tsp ground cinnamon (you can add a little extra)
1/2 cup raisins (I add more)

Preparation
Preheat oven to 375 degrees. Boil noodles in salted water for about 4 minutes then strain. In a large mixing bowl, combine noodles with all remaining ingredients and pour into a greased, approximately 9-by-13-inch, baking dish. Bake until custard is set and top is golden, about 30 to 45 minutes.

29. Karen's Luchen Kugel
Submitted by Karen Shuffler

Ingredients
8 ounces egg noodles (yolk free can be used)
8 ounces low-fat cottage cheese (1 cup)
8 ounces low-fat sour cream (1 cup)
4 tablespoons unsalted butter/margarine (1/2 stick) melted
2 large eggs

½ cup granulated sugar (a little less is OK)
1 teaspoon vanilla extract
¼ teaspoon salt
1 ½ cups skim milk
¾ cup of dried apricots cut up (optional). Some people use raisins or currants (both optional)

Preparation
Heat oven to 350 and arrange a rack in the middle. Bring a large pot of salted water to a boil over high heat. Add noodles. Stir and cook until al dente or according to package directions. Drain & set aside. Place cottage cheese, sour cream, butter/margarine, eggs, sugar, vanilla and measured salt in a large bowl and whisk until evenly combined. Add the noodles and stir until incorporated. Pour the mixture into a greased 13x9 inch baking dish and spread evenly. Pour the milk all over the top. Bake for 1 hour (should be golden brown on top). Serves 8. Can be eaten warm, room temperature or cold.

30. Sweet Noodle Kugel from Diane
Submitted by Diane Dubey

Ingredients
1 pound wide egg noodles
½ cup butter (healthy version, ⅙ cup)
1 cup whole milk (healthy version, low fat)
4 large eggs (yolks are healthy and give texture to your kugel)
¾ cup sugar (healthy version, ½ cup)
2½ teaspoons vanilla
1 teaspoon salt
1-pound container sour cream or Greek yogurt
1-pound container cottage cheese

Topping ingredients:
3 cups crushed cornflakes
3 T sugar
1½ teaspoon cinnamon
3 T soft butter, cut into bits

Preparation
Preheat to 350 degrees F. Butter a 9x13x2 inch glass or ceramic dish and set aside. Cook noodles according to directions until al dente. Drain well, then return to the pot and add the amount of butter of your choosing, totally coating the noodles. Mix together milk, eggs, sugar, vanilla, and salt. Then stir in sour cream or Greek yogurt. Lastly, mix in cottage cheese. Combine your noodles with the mixture, and transfer into the dish. To make the topping, toss together cornflakes, sugar, cinnamon and butter and sprinkle evenly over noodles. Bake kugel for 1 hour until golden brown. Let stand at least 5-10 minutes before serving. Serve warm or at room temperature.

31. Sweet Noodle Kugel from Suzanne
Submitted by Suzanne Hilary

Ingredients
1 lb. egg noodles (curly ones are best)
1 stick butter
8 oz. cream cheese
8 oz. sour cream
6 eggs, slightly beaten
1 t. vanilla
1 c. sugar
8 oz. can of crushed pineapple (do not drain)
1 jar of jam or marmalade (apricot, peach or orange)

For top:
1 cup of any crunchy cereal
¼ c. sugar
2 t. cinnamon
4 T. butter

Preparation
Boil noodles according to the package directions. Combine butter, cream, sour cream, eggs, vanilla and sugar and beat well with an electric mixer. Drain noodles and let cool slightly (don't rinse). Combine sour cream mix, noodles, pineapple and jam/marmalade in another bowl, then combine noodles and this mixture. Put mixture in a buttered 13x9 glass dish. Cover with foil and let sit in the refrigerator for at least 4 hours or overnight. THIS STEP IS VERY IMPORTANT.

Preheat oven to 350 degrees. Sprinkle dry topping items over kugel. Dot the butter on top. Bake for one hour or until golden brown.

32. Sweet-Crunchy Kugel
Submitted by Diane Dubey currently residing in Lincolnwood, Il.

<u>Ingredients</u>
2 8-ounce packages low-fat cream cheese or Neufchâtel cheese, softened
8 tablespoons butter, at room temperature
3/4 to 1 cup sugar
8 large eggs
4 cups nonfat milk
1/3 cup low-fat sour cream plus sour cream for serving
1/3 cup cottage cheese
2 teaspoons ground cinnamon
2 teaspoons vanilla extract
12 ounces medium or wide egg noodles
2 cups frosted flakes cereal

<u>Preparation</u>
Lightly grease an 11-by-16-inch baking dish with nonstick cooking spray. Mix the cream cheese or Neufchâtel cheese, butter, and sugar in the bowl of a standing mixer, blending on medium speed for a few minutes, then add the eggs one at a time, incorporating after each addition. Reduce the speed to low, add the milk, sour cream, cottage cheese, cinnamon and vanilla extract; the mixture will be very wet.

Bring a pot of water to a boil and add the uncooked noodles and simmer, uncovered for about 5 minutes. Drain, run under cold water, drain again and incorporate into the wet mixture. Pour the cream cheese mixture and noodle mixture into the baking pan. The noodles should be just about covered with the mixture; cover and refrigerate a few hours or overnight.

Bake uncovered in a 350° oven for 40 minutes. Take the kugel out of the oven and lightly crush handfuls of cereal over the top, spreading the cereal evenly. Return to the oven and bake 20 minutes more, or until light to medium brown around the edges and no longer have liquid inside. Shake the pan to see if the kugel seems solid.

33. Coconut Noodle Kugel
Submitted by Candy Rathsmill
From Debbie Bashoff

Ingredients
½ lb. fine noodles
3 c. whole milk
4 eggs
2 t. vanilla
½ stick sweet butter
½-¾ c. coconut
1 c. sugar

Preparation
Boil noodles until done. Butter a 9x13 glass dish. In a blender, mix the eggs and ½ c. milk slowly. Add the remaining milk, sugar and vanilla, and blend again. Melt butter and drizzle on top. Sprinkle coconut above everything. Bake for 1 hour and 10 minutes at 350 degrees.

34. Noodle Kugel with Candied Pecans
Submitted by Diane Dubey

Ingredients
1 pound wide egg noodles
½ cup butter, plus more for buttering pan
1 cup whole milk
4 large eggs
¾ cup sugar
2½ teaspoons vanilla
1 teaspoon salt
1-pound container sour cream
1-pound container cottage cheese
½ cup raisins (optional)

Topping:
3 T butter, softened
3 T brown sugar

1 teaspoon ground cinnamon
1 cup chopped pecans (or walnuts), chopped or whole

Preparation
Preheat oven to 350 degrees F. Butter a 13x9-inch glass or ceramic dish. The dish should be at least 2 inches deep. Cook noodles in salted water according to package directions until al dente. Drain well and then return the noodles to the pot. Add butter and gently mix to melt, completely coating the noodles. In a large bowl, whisk together milk, eggs, sugar, vanilla, and salt. Then stir in sour cream, cottage cheese, and raisins. Combine your noodles with the mixture, and transfer into the baking dish.

To make the topping, stir together butter, brown sugar, cinnamon, and nuts in a small bowl. Sprinkle evenly over kugel. Bake kugel for 1 hour until golden brown. Let stand at least 5-10 minutes before serving. Serve warm or at room temperature.

35. Noodle Pudding from Renee
Submitted by Renee Sokol from Bethlehem, Pa.

Ingredients
1 lb. noodles
1 stick melted oleo
1 cup sugar
4 eggs
1 can crushed pineapple
1 can sliced peaches (drained)

Preparation
Cook and drain noodles. Mix all ingredients in a bowl. Bake in a greased baking dish for 45 minutes at 375 degrees.

Enjoy!

36. Pumpkin Noodle Kugel
Submitted by Diane Dubey

<u>Ingredients</u>
1 12-oz package fettuccine, cooked according to package instructions
4 eggs
¾ cup pumpkin puree
½ cup maple syrup or honey
2 T bourbon
1 teaspoon vanilla extract
1 teaspoon cinnamon
½ teaspoon ground ginger
Pinch of cloves

Crumb Topping:
1½ cups graham cracker crumbs
½ cup brown sugar
1 teaspoon cinnamon
1T oil
1 T bourbon

<u>Preparation</u>
Preheat your oven to 350 degrees. Grease a 9x13 pan and set aside. In a large bowl, combine cooked fettuccine, eggs, pumpkin puree, maple syrup, bourbon, vanilla, cinnamon, ginger, and cloves. Stir mixture until everything is evenly distributed. Pour mixture into prepared pan and set aside.

Prepare crumbs:
Combine all crumb ingredients in a small bowl, stir until all crumbs have been dampened. Spread mixture over the prepared noodle mixture in pan. Bake at 350 degrees for about an hour, until crumbs are golden, and kugel feels firm.

37. Fran's Delicious Noodle Kugel
Submitted by Fran Sherman

Ingredients
½ lb. wide noodles
2 eggs
½ stick butter,
3 slices American cheese
4 oz. can of crushed pineapple
½ cup sugar
½ cup milk
3 T. sour cream
3 oz. brick cream cheese
¼ t. salt
Any brand of grape nut flakes crushed
Cinnamon

Preparation
Cook noodles, drain. In a bowl, beat eggs. Stir in melted butter and American cheese. Add crushed pineapple, stir. Add remaining ingredients except Grape Nut Flakes and cinnamon, stir. Add in cooked noodles. Grease a 9 or 10 inch baking dish. Pour mixture into dish. Sprinkle top lightly with crushed Grape Nut Flakes mixed with cinnamon. Bake at 350° for 1 hour.

38. Mom's Famous Noodle Pudding
Submitted by Jude Brownstein
This recipe is from her Aunt Fran Hearst. She and Jude's Mom, Mimi Canton, always kidded one another as to who found the recipe first. She said that her mothers was sensational. She didn't use raisins. Don't forget the vanilla.

Ingredients
1 lb. extra wide noodles
1 1/2 cups sugar
8 eggs
1/2 lb. lightly salted butter
1 tsp. vanilla
1 pint cottage cheese

1 pint sour cream
2 cups milk
1 1/2 cups golden raisins
1 small (single-serving size) box of cornflakes, crushed
Cinnamon/Sugar

Preparation
Grease a large baking pan (approx. 10 x 13) with butter. Boil and drain noodles. Add these ingredients to noodles in a large bowl or pot: butter, sugar, cottage cheese, sour cream, vanilla and, if used, raisins. MIX WELL. Pour into a greased pan. Beat the eggs and milk together and mix well; pour this mixture over the noodle mixture. Crush one small, single-serving box of Corn Flakes. Sprinkle crushed corn flakes on top; then, sprinkle cinnamon/sugar condiment on top of the entire pudding. (NOTE: Jude also adds a bit of the
cinnamon/sugar into the noodles). Bake at 350 degrees for 1-1 1/2 hours. Eat hot or cooled. Sinfully Delicious! Enjoy!

39. Francyn's Noodle Kugel
Submitted by Julie Einstein currently residing in Centennial, Co.
This recipe is from her Mom, Francyne Greenberg

Ingredients
1 bag noodles
1 can crushed pineapple
1 ½ sticks butter
2 cups sugar
5 beaten eggs

Preparation
Spray pan. Boil noodles. Drain. Add butter, eggs, sugar and pineapple. Stir together. Put in the oven at 350 degrees for 1 ½ hours.

40. Jill's Sweet Kugel
Submitted by Jill Yuter Max of Elkins Park, Pa.
Jill stated that this recipe can also be made at Passover exchanging one pound of farfel for the noodles

Ingredients
1 pound medium egg noodles, boiled/drained
1 pound cottage cheese
1 cup sour cream
2 T. vanilla
2 T. cinnamon (mix in with noodles, sprinkle on top)
1 can pineapple tidbits, drained
1 ½ cups sugar
6 eggs
1 stick melted butter

Preparation
Mix all together. Bake at 350 degrees in a lasagna sized pan, uncovered, for 45-60 minutes.

41. Rhonda's Family Cheese Kugel
Submitted by Rhonda Feuer
A family favorite cheesecake style recipe from Shirley Yorra

Ingredients
16 oz. cream cheese
1 pint sour cream
½ lb. butter, melted
1 small can of evaporated milk
4 eggs, separated, beat well
1 c, sugar
12 oz. fine noodles, cooked 4 minutes
1 t. vanilla
1 t. salt

Preparation
Beat egg yolks with sugar. Add all of the other ingredients except the egg whites. Gradually add the egg whites with the cooked noodles. Pour into a buttered pan. Cook at 350 degrees for 45-60 minutes.

42. Naomi's Easy Yerushalayim Kugel
Submitted by Ima Audrey

Ingredients
1 box thin spaghetti pasta
3/4 box dark brown sugar
1/3 cup oil
3 eggs
1 1/2 black pepper
1 tsp salt

Preparation
Boil pasta until al dente. Mix all the ingredients with the pasta. Bake 350 degrees uncovered till done.

43. Apple Honey Raisin Noodle Kugel
Submitted by Ima Audrey

Ingredients
12 ounce wide egg noodles.
1/2 stick melted margarine
4 apples
3/4 cup golden raisins (optional)
1/3 cup sugar
1/4 cup honey
1 and 1/2 tsp cinnamon
Pinch salt
5 large eggs

Preparation
Grease a 9x13 baking dish or pan. Cook the noodles until al dente. Drain them and return them to the cooking pot and add the melted margarine. Mix well and set aside to cool. Peel the apples, cut them in quarters. Remove the core and seeds and slice the apples into the noodles. Add the raisins, cinnamon, sugar and honey. Mix well. Gently beat the eggs together and blend into the noodle mixture. Pour into the greased pan. Cover kugel. Put in a preheated 350° oven. Bake for 30 minutes. Remove the foil and bake for another 20 minutes or until golden brown.

44. Donna's Spinach Noodle Kugel
Submitted by Debbie Cotton

Ingredients
1 (16-oz) pkg. fine egg noodles
1 (16-oz) container cottage cheese
2 1/2 c. shredded mozzarella cheese
1 tsp. chopped onion
2 pkg. frozen spinach souffle, thawed

Preparation
Mix noodles, cheeses and onion. Pour into a greased 13x9 baking dish. Bake at 350 degrees for 15 minutes. Remove from the oven and top with thawed spinach. Bake an additional 45 minutes until firm.

45. Grandma K's Kugel
Submitted by Lee Dame-Gordon
Lee says it is a foolproof kugel recipe. A neighbor had made it for her family after her mom had surgery years and years ago

Ingredients
1 lb. bag of noodles
1 lb. cottage cheese 2%
1 pint low-fat vanilla yogurt
1 stick melted butter
6 jumbo eggs
1 capful vanilla
1 cup sugar

3 tsp. cinnamon
A little extra dash of sugar

Boil 1 lb. bag of noodles and drain. Combine with cottage cheese. Mix with drained noodles. Spray a 9x13 pan with nonstick cooking spray. Pour ingredients in. Sprinkle cornflake crumbs mixed with cinnamon over the entire top of pan Dot with additional butter. Bake 55-60 minutes at 350° until the knife inserted comes out clean.

46. Estee's Luckshen Kugel
Submitted by Estee Glazer

Ingredients
1 lb. broad noodles
1 pt. sour cream
1 lb. cottage cheese
1 c. milk
½ tsp. salt
6 T. sugar
6 T. melted butter
crushed cornflakes

Preparation
Preheat oven to 350 degrees F (180 degrees C). Cook noodles according to package directions. Drain and rinse well. Mix with sour cream, cottage cheese, milk, salt, sugar and melted butter. Place in a greased 9x13 baking dish. Top with crushed cornflakes and dot with 2 T. (30 ml) butter. Bake for 1½ hours.

To freeze: Freeze uncooked, well wrapped, and bring to room temperature before baking.

47. Aunt Mickey's Kugel
Submitted by Sheryl Wachtel Cutler

Ingredients
8 oz. medium egg noodles
8 oz. cream cheese
1 stick margarine

½ c. sugar
4 eggs
1 c. milk
1 tsp. vanilla
½ c. golden raisins or dried cranberries
Sugar covered cornflakes (double bag and use a rolling pan to crush)
Cinnamon

Preparation
Preheat oven to 350°. Cook noodles and set aside. Using a hand mixer, mix cream cheese, margarine and sugar together. Mix in the eggs, milk and raisins. Stir in noodles. Pour into a greased 2 quart casserole. Cover with crushed flakes and sprinkle with cinnamon (you may want to add the cinnamon to the bag while crushing the sweet, sugary cornflakes. It distributes the flavor better). Bake at 350° for 1 to 1¼ hours.

48. Elayne's Noodle Kugel
Submitted by Elayne Rose currently residing in Vernon Hills, Il.
From her sister Sandra Sabin

Ingredients
1 8-ounce package wide noodles, cooked and drained
½ cup butter
Salt
1 8-ounce package of cream cheese
6 tablespoons sugar
4 eggs beaten
1¾ cup milk
Sugary cornflakes

Preparation
Cream butter and cream cheese. Add salt, sugar and eggs. Gradually add milk and blend. Stir in noodles (mixture will be very liquid). Pour into a greased 13x9 inch baking dish. Bake at 350 for 45-60 minutes. About 30 minutes into baking, add crumbled cornflakes to the top of the kugel and continue baking. Enjoy.

49. Flora's Noodle Kugel
Submitted by Gwen Federman
Flora was like an aunt to her mother. Her grandmother and Flora were good friends and next-door neighbors on Friendship Street in Philadelphia, PA. where her mom grew up

<u>Ingredients</u>
½ -1 lb. fine noodles
8 eggs, at room temperature
1-pint sour cream, room temperature
8 oz. cream cheese, at room temperature
2 tsp. vanilla
1 c. sugar
½ lb. margarine, melted
Cinnamon sugar for topping

<u>Preparation</u>
Cook noodles, drain, but reserve some cooking liquid to loosen noodles when you are ready to mix with the wet ingredients. Preheat oven to 350 degrees Fahrenheit. Beat eggs, sour cream, cream cheese, sugar, and margarine in a mixer for 15 minutes. Grease a 9x13 baking pan. Mix wet ingredients with noodles and mix thoroughly. Pour into greased baking pan. Sprinkle cinnamon on top and bake for one hour. Cool at room temperature, slightly, before serving.

50. Aunt Debbie's Kugel
Submitted by Barb Rosenstock
Recipe is from her sister-in-law, her children's Aunt Debbie

<u>Ingredients</u>
4 eggs, beaten
1 lb. wide egg noodles, cooked
1 c. sugar
1 stick melted butter
1 can crushed pineapple, drained
½ c. applesauce
½ c. cottage cheese
½ c. cornflake crumbs
1t. cinnamon

1T. sugar

Preparation
Combine all ingredients except crumbs, cinnamon and sugar in a bowl and mix. Pour mixture into a greased 9x13 pan. Sprinkle with the crumbs, cinnamon and sugar. Bake at 350° for 1 hour and 15 minutes.

51. Grammie Shirley's Prize Winning Noodle Kugel
Submitted by Michelle Levine

Ingredients
½ c. butter or margarine
1 ½ c. brown sugar
1 lb. wide noodles
3 eggs
½ c. sour cream
1 tsp. vanilla
Slivered almonds or chopped pecans
3 qt. circular mold pan (12 c.)

Preparation
Soften butter and blend in 1 cup of brown sugar. Cook noodles in salted water until tender. Drain well. Beat eggs, mix with sour cream, vanilla, and remaining brown sugar. Add to noodles. With hands, spread brown sugar and butter combination on bottom and side of mold. Press almonds or chopped pecans on bottom and sides. Pour in noodle mixture. Bake in preheated 350° oven for 1 hour. Serves 8.

52. Noodle Pudding from Sarna's Great Grandmother
Submitted by Sarna Lee Goldenberg
Sarna's great grandmother, Bella, entered a contest with this kugel recipe and won a new oven, back in the 1930's

Ingredients
1 lb. pkg. broad noodles
6 eggs
½ cup sugar

1 tsp. cinnamon
½ cup honey
½ lb. butter
1 cup seedless YELLOW raisins
¾ cup chopped pecans
2 apples, pared and diced

Preparation
Cook noodles per instructions on pkg. and drain well. Beat eggs well. Add to noodles with seasonings, ¼ lb. of the butter, fruit, nuts and honey. Reserve some honey, cinnamon and nuts. Mix well. Grease a 3 qt. (9x13) baking dish with ¼ lb. butter and fill with noodle mixture. Sprinkle with remaining cinnamon, nuts and honey. Pour some melted butter on top. Bake 1 hour in a 350-degree oven. Serves at least 16 persons.

53. Leslie's Noodle Kugel
Submitted by Leslie Berland Freedman

Ingredients
8-16 ounces of broad egg noodles
5 T. melted butter
6 eggs
½ cup sugar
6 oz. cream cheese, softened
4T. sour cream
1 lb. creamy cottage cheese, small curd

For the topping
⅔ cup graham cracker crumbs (Leslie like cinnamon graham cracker crumbs)
½ cup sugar
1 stick melted butter

Preparation
Cook noodles according to the package directions and drain well. Pour into a large bowl. Mix in melted butter and set aside. Beat eggs with sugar and cream cheese. Mix into noodles. Stir in sour cream and cottage cheese. Pour into a greased 9x13 pan. Combine topping ingredients. Sprinkle over kugel. Bake for 1 hour at 350 degrees.

54. Noodle Kugel with Pineapples
Submitted by Alysia Miller-Goldstein

Ingredients
1 bag of no yolk noodles
½-⅓ c. sugar
1 can of drained pineapple
Cornflake crumbs
Cinnamon
A sprinkle more of sugar

Preparation
Preheat the oven to 350 degrees. Cook the noodles per package directions. Drain and add the sugar and the pineapples. Mix together and pour into the pan. Cover with the cornflake crumbs, cinnamon and sugar. Bake for 45-60 minutes.

55. One-Step Noodle Kugel
Submitted by Sue Ulman

Ingredients
1 stick margarine
3 eggs, beaten
2 c. milk
½ c. sugar
1 tsp. vanilla
8 oz. small curd cottage cheese
8 oz. medium noodles, uncooked
15-20 oz. crushed pineapple, with juice
⅓ c. raisins
Crushed cornflakes for topping (not crumbs)

Preparation
Melt margarine in a 9x13x2 inch glass baking dish at 350°. Mix eggs, milk, sugar, vanilla, cottage cheese, uncooked noodles, melted margarine, pineapple and raisins in a large bowl. Stir well with a fork. Pour into dish that margarine was melted in. Press noodles under liquid with

a fork. Sprinkle with cornflakes. Bake one hour at 350°. Cut in squares or slices. Can be frozen and reheated.

56. Hodge Podge Kugel
Submitted by Diane Roberts

Ingredients
1 lb. noodles, cooked and drained
8 oz. farmer cheese
1 stick butter
2 ½ c. milk
8 oz. softened cream cheese
2 onions, sauteed
2 sauteed mushrooms
Pistachio nuts, roasted and chopped
½ c. dried fruit
2 hard boiled eggs, chopped

Preparation
Mix everything together. Bake at 350 degrees with foil on top for 30 minutes. Take the foil off and bake for an additional 30 minutes.

57. Barbara's Noodle Pudding
Submitted by my Aunt Roslyn Braun
This is a recipe from her former coworker, Barbara Morris

Ingredients
1 lb. wide egg noodles
1 c. sugar
6 beaten eggs
16 oz. large curd cottage cheese
1 pt. sour cream
8 oz. cream cheese
1 stick melted butter
¼ c. mixed cinnamon sugar

Preparation
Grease a 9x13 glass or ceramic pan and preheat the oven to 325 for glass and 350 degrees for all other pans. Cook noodles "al dente" and cool. Beat eggs and sugar for 2 minutes. Add cream cheese and beat until fairly smooth (there will be some lumps). Add cottage cheese, sour cream and melted butter. Add noodles and mix to incorporate. Pour into the pan and sprinkle with cinnamon sugar.

Optional items can be added to the mixture before baking: raisins, slivered almonds, fruit salad, or crushed pineapple, drained.

Bake for 1 hour and 5 minutes. If you want to bake one day and use it 1-2 days later, bake for the longer time and refrigerate.

58. Artichoke and Brie Kugel Bites
Submitted by Fern Kohn

Ingredients
12 oz. wide noodles
2 cans artichoke hearts, drained
Large triangle of brie (remove crust and cut into small pieces)
8 egg whites
6 oz. yogurt
½ c. buttermilk
8 oz. flavored cream cheese
2 cloves of garlic, minced
Salt and pepper

For topping:
½ stick butter or margarine
1 ½ cups shredded mozzarella cheese (¾ for kugel, ¾ for topping)
1 ½ c. corn flake crumbs

Preparation
Cook noodles according to package directions. Combine the artichoke hearts, brie, egg whites, yogurt, buttermilk, garlic and ¾ c. of the mozzarella cheese. Blend together well. Fold in the noodles, and make sure they also are blended well. Spoon the kugel mixture into 2 trays (24)

of well greased muffin tins. Combine all of the ingredients for topping and blend together well. Bake uncovered in a preheated 375-degree oven for 25 minutes.

59. Bubbie Florence's Kugel
Submitted by sisters Jill, Shelley, and Stacey Sevelow
This recipe comes from their Bubbie Florence, who passed it down to her daughter, Gussie, who passed it down to her daughters

Ingredients
1 package extra wide egg noodles
3-4 extra large eggs
¾ cup sugar
⅔ cup canola oil
2 t. vanilla
optional: add raisins at Rosh Hashanah

Preparation
Cook noodles according to the directions. Beat eggs, add the rest of the ingredients; pour noodles in. Pour into a 3-quart shatterproof glass dish. Bake at 350 degrees for one hour, until top noodles are nice and brown without burning.

60. Family Kugel Recipe from Tracy
Submitted by Tracy Glass Teitelbaum

Ingredients
12 oz. wide noodles
6 eggs
1 lb. small curd cottage cheese
3 oz. cream cheese
¼ lb. butter
1 c. sour cream
¾ c. sugar
1 t. vanilla
Raisins are optional

Blend everything except the noodles in a food processor until liquid. Mix in raisins.

Topping:
1 c. graham cracker crumbs
½ c. brown sugar
¼ c. melted butter
Cinnamon to taste (at least a couple of teaspoons)

Preparation
Mix everything together by hand. Put noodles in a 9x13 greased glass dish. Pour mixture over and mix a little. Sprinkle topping on top. Bake at 350° for 45 minutes.

61. Noodle Kugel with Peas and Parmesan
Submitted by Stan Kruper

Ingredients
16 oz. wide egg noodles, cooked, drained
1 stick butter
1 c. milk
5 eggs
1 c. frozen peas
32 oz. small curd cottage cheese
5 T. sour cream
½ t. salt
½ t. pepper
1 c. onions, sautéed
1 c. parmesan cheese

Preparation
Preheat the oven to 350°. Place a stick of butter or margarine in a 13x9 inch pan and let it melt. In a large mixing bowl, combine the milk, eggs, cottage cheese and sour cream. Season with salt and pepper. Add the peas and onions. Next, add the noodle mixture to the mixture in the bowl. Blend well. Pour into pan and cook for one hour.

62. Lokshen Kugel from Lynda
Submitted by Lynda Hirsekorn
Made it for Rosh Hashana and everybody loved it

Ingredients
Butter (for the dish)
Salt, to taste
1 pound medium or wide egg noodles
1 pint (2 cups) sour cream
1 cup golden raisins
1/2 cup (1 stick) unsalted butter, cut up
1 pound (2 cups) small curd cottage cheese
1 package (7.5 ounces) farmer cheese
1 cup sugar
2 teaspoons vanilla
8 eggs, beaten to mix
1 jar (12 ounces) apricot preserves
1 teaspoon ground cinnamon mixed with 2 tablespoons sugar (for sprinkling)

Preparation
Set oven at 350 degrees. Butter a 9-by-13-inch baking dish. Bring a large pot of salted water to a boil. Add the noodles and cook, stirring occasionally, for 8 minutes or until they are tender but still have some bite (they should be slightly underdone because they'll cook more later). In a bowl, combine the sour cream and raisins; set aside for 10 minutes. Drain the noodles into a colander and return them to the pot. Add the butter and stir well. Stir in the cottage cheese, farmer cheese, sugar, vanilla, a large pinch of salt, eggs, and sour cream mixture. Pour half the noodle mixture into the baking dish. Add the apricot preserves in spoonfuls here and there. Top with the remaining noodle mixture. Sprinkle with cinnamon-sugar. Bake the Kugel for 1 to 1 1/4 hours or until the mixture is set.

63. Noodle Kugel from Nancy
Submitted by Vicki Herrick
Recipe from her cousin Nancy Margolis

Ingredients
One pkg of noodles- 12oz
6 oz cottage cheese
6 oz sour cream
4 eggs
1/4 lb. melted butter
3/4 cup sugar
1/2 cup corn flakes

Preparation
Melt butter in a glass dish. Cook noodles. Combine all ingredients including melted butter leaving out 1/4 corn flakes and mix with a mixer. Pour into baking dish and top with crushed corn flakes. Cook for 45 minutes to 1 hour at 350 degrees. Enjoy.

64. Yummy Kugel
Submitted by Barbara Dolinger currently residing in Highland Park, Il.

Ingredients
1 lb noodles
1/2 lb butter
1 1/2 cups sugar
3/4 cup cold milk
4 well beaten eggs
2 caps lemon juice
1 1/2 vanilla extract
Cinnamon

Preparation
Mix together noodles (which have been cooked al dente), butter and sugar while the noodles are still hot. Add cold milk. Add the beaten eggs, lemon juice, and vanilla. Sprinkle with cinnamon. Place in a greased baking dish and bake for 1 hour at 325 degrees.

Barbara states that sometimes the top gets too crispy, so she bakes it covered for some of the time.

65. Bea's Noodle Kugel
Submitted by Holly Hollander from Los, Angeles, Ca.
Holly stated that her mom was not a good cook, but this is delish!! Many folks think this is dessert, but not Holly! She usually cuts the sugar and butter and makes most of the ingredients low or non-fat

Ingredients
8 oz wide noodles
3 eggs
3/4 c milk
3/4 c sour cream
1/2 c butter
1/2 c sugar
2 tsp almond extract

Preparation
Cook noodles al dente. Mix all of the other ingredients together in a large bowl and then add drained cooked noodles. Mix. Put into 8x8 in a baking dish and bake at 350 degrees until golden brown, about 1 hour.

This can be made leaner with low or non-fat ingredients and/or less butter and sugar. It also can be successfully doubled or tripled. The almond extract is what makes it special, but you can substitute vanilla.

66. Kate's Noodle Kugel
Submitted by Kate Smith

Ingredients
1 lb. fine egg noodles
¼ lb. melted butter
1 lb. cottage cheese
5 eggs (4, plus 1 for topping)
1 pint sour cream

1 ½ c. milk (½ plus 1 for topping)
1 c. sugar
1 t. vanilla
1 t. salt
1 c. sugary cornflakes

Preparation
Preheat oven to 375. Grease a large pan. Cook and drain noodles. Mix cooked noodles with butter, cottage cheese, 4 eggs, sour cream, ½ c. milk, vanilla, sugar and salt. Pour into pan. Beat egg and 1 c. milk and pour over noodle mixture. Cover top with crushed sugary cornflakes. Bake for 1 hour. Serves 12.

67. Skinny Noodle Kugel
Submitted by Bruce Pearl

Ingredients
1 lb. FINE thin noodles
1 qt. 2% milk
1 lb. cottage cheese
½ lb. cream cheese softened
6 eggs
2 tsp. vanilla
1 stick drawn butter & a little extra for drizzle
1 cup golden raisins
1 ¼ cup sugar (a bit more if you flavor sweet) plus extra for top sprinkle
Graham cracker crumbs

Preparation
In a large bowl mix cottage cheese, cream cheese and milk. Add beaten eggs, sugar and vanilla. Stir well and then add melted butter. Boil noodles until al dente and drain. Mix into mixture. Add raisins and mix all. Place in a well greased 11x13 lasagna pan. It will fill to the top. Sprinkle with graham cracker crumbs, a bit of sugar and some melted butter. Bake at 350° for 55-65 minutes until golden and bubbly. It should be a bit moist but not wet and runny. Let rest for 30 minutes.

Serves 12-15. May be served warm or cold and may be frozen.

68. Tasty Noodle Pudding
Submitted by Mark Macklin currently residing in Albuquerque, NM
Recipe from his mother, Ellen Macklin

Ingredients
8 oz. medium egg noodles
6 oz. cream cheese
6 T. margarine
3 large eggs
½ cup sugar
¾ cup milk
1 cup apricot nectar

Topping (optional)
5 T. margarine, melted
1 cup cornflake crumbs
½ cup sugar
½ t. cinnamon

Preparation
Preheat oven to 350°. Cook and drain the noodles. Return the noodles to the pot and add the cream cheese and margarine. Toss until the cheese and margarine until melted. Place the mixture into a 7x11 inch glass baking dish. Combine the eggs, sugar, milk and apricot nectar. Pour over the noodles and mix. Sprinkle with the topping combination if desired. Bake for 45 minutes. Let stand 5-10 minutes before serving. Yield: 8 servings.

69. Fabulous Noodle Kugel
Submitted by Terri Harris

Ingredients
1 lb broad noodles, cooked and drained
1 cup sugar
1 lb cottage cheese
1-1/2 tsp vanilla
1 cup white raisins, optional
7 eggs beaten

3 cups milk
1 pint of sour cream
1/4 lb butter, melted

Preparation
Mix all pudding ingredients together in a large bowl. Consistency will be loose. Add cooked noodles. Pour into two greased pans (each 13x9). Bake at 350 degrees for 1-1/2 hours or until golden brown on top. If desired, top with cinnamon or 1/2 cup cornflakes crumbled with 1 tsp cinnamon and 1 tsp sugar

70. Especially on Shavuot Noodle Kugel
Submitted by Melissa Kaufman
Made especially on Shavuot by her Aunt Bonita who learned it from her Bubbie Sarah

15-minute prep time and cook time is approx. 1 hour.

Ingredients
1 cup raisins (optional) - you may substitute other fruits like craisins, dried chopped apricots, or chopped drained pineapple
12 oz wide egg noodles
6 large eggs
1 lb sour cream (2 cups)
8 oz cottage cheese (1 cup)
8 oz cream cheese, softened - OR farmer's cheese, crumbled (1 cup)
1 cup sugar
1/4 cup unsalted butter, melted
1/4 tsp salt
cinnamon and sugar for dusting
nonstick cooking oil spray

Preparation
Recipe will call for you to use: a large pot, food processor or blender, 9x13 baking dish

Place a rack in the middle of your oven and preheat to 350 degrees F. Cover the raisins with hot water and let them soak to plump while you prepare the other ingredients. Bring a large pot of water to a boil. Add the noodles to the pot, bring back to a boil, and let them cook until tender (not overly soft), about 5 minutes. Drain and return the cooked noodles to the pot. In a food processor or blender, blend together the eggs, sour cream, cottage cheese, cream cheese, sugar, melted butter, and salt. Pour the egg mixture over the cooked noodles in the pot and stir until well combined. Drain the raisins. Stir them into the noodles.

Spray a 9x13 inch baking dish with nonstick cooking oil. Pour the noodle mixture into the dish. Top the kugel by sprinkling generously with sugar and lightly with cinnamon. Alternatively, you can use your favorite kugel topping (streusel, crushed graham crackers, cornflakes, etc.).

Bake the kugel for about 60 minutes, turning once halfway through cooking, till the center of the kugel is set and the tips of the noodles turn golden brown. Remove from the oven. Let the kugel rest for 15-20 minutes before slicing. Kugel can be served warm or cold.

71. Laura Sherman's Sweet Lockshen Kugel
Submitted by Cathy Sherman Ostrow from Gilbertsville, Pa.

Ingredients
1 cup raisins, either golden or dark
12 oz. wide egg noodles
6 large eggs
16 oz. sour cream
8 oz. cottage cheese
¼ cup orange juice or Grand Marnier (mom's secret weapon for blintz crepe and kugel)
Sweeten with sugar to taste
¼ cup unsalted butter, melted
¼ t. salt
Cinnamon and sugar for dusting, dot with butter

Preparation
Cook the noodles according to package directions. Butter the pan. Pour in all of the ingredients. Bake at 350 degrees for an hour.

72. Noodle Kugel from Mt. Kisco, N.Y.
Submitted by Edith Shore

Ingredients
1 8oz pkg broad noodles, boiled & drained
1 lb creamed cottage cheese
1 stick butter
3 eggs
1c sugar
1 pint sour cream
1 tsp vanilla
Sugar & cinnamon mixture stirred together with cornflakes crumbs

Preparation
Mix all ingredients (except cinnamon sugar and cornflakes crumbs) together. Pour into a greased 9x11 pan. Top with a generous amount of sugar, cinnamon and cornflakes crumbs. Bake at 350 degrees for 1 1/2 hours. Serve hot.

73. Applesauce Noodle Kugel
Submitted by Todd Freer
Recipe is from his Mom, Ruth Freer

Ingredients
8 oz broad noodles
4 eggs, slightly beaten
1/2 cup sugar
1 pint sour cream
1/4 cup raisins
1 16 oz jar applesauce
Cinnamon
Salt
Butter

Preparation
Cook and drain the noodles. Mix all the ingredients together. Dot with butter in a greased 8x8 baking dish. Bake in a preheated oven at 350 degrees for one hour. Can be doubled.

74. Noodle Kugel from Sharona
Submitted by Sharona Blochs
From her dear Aunt Maxine Cohn

<u>Ingredients</u>
1 lb. broad noodles, cooked and drained
6 eggs
8 oz. cream cheese
1 ½ c. cottage cheese
Beat all together

16 oz. applesauce
1 c. raisins (optional)
½ c. sugar
1 t. cinnamon
Mix all together

½ c. melted butter
½ c. brown sugar
½ c. crushed pecans (optional)
Put on bottom of large pan
1 can cherry or apple pie filling (optional)

<u>Preparation</u>
Put brown sugar mixture on the bottom of the pan. Mix all of the above ingredients together and place on top of the bottom layer. Cover and cook at 375 degrees for one hour. Uncover the fruit pie filling on top and cook for 30 minutes more. Serves 14 people.

75. Kimberly's Luckshen Kugel
Submitted by Carrie Shoen of Yonkers, NY
Recipe from Kimberly Niehaus

<u>Ingredients</u>
3 large eggs
8 oz. egg noodles
¼ c. butter, softened (or up to ½ c. if you want more butter)

1 lb. cottage cheese
Salt and pepper to taste

Preparation
Cook and drain noodles. Beat eggs well, add cottage cheese, butter, noodles, salt and pepper. Mix well. Pour into a 9x9 baking dish and bake for about 40 minutes until the tops are browning a bit and the sides are pulling away. Err on the side of over, rather than under baking. The crunchy noodles on the top are the best.

76. Estelle's Spinach Noodle Kugel
Submitted by Sharona Blochs
From Estelle Limer

Ingredients
2 packs of defrosted chopped spinach
1 lb. med. noodles–cooked and drained
1 envelope onion soup mix
1 stick margarine/butter melted
3 eggs
1 cup nondairy coffee creamer
A little evaporated milk

Preparation
Bake in a 9x13 inch pan for 45 min at 350° uncovered.

77. Noodle Kugel from Marion
Submitted by Marion Perkins from Nuremberg, Germany, currently residing in Vernon Hills, Il.
This recipe is from her Auntie Shelly (Rochelle Berger), who has since passed away and Marion misses her so much............food connects people and this recipe really does it for her!

Ingredients
1 lb wide noodles
2 sticks of butter (toss with warm noodles)
6 beaten eggs

1 lb cottage cheese
1 lb sour cream
3 apples sliced in small pieces
1 C golden raisins
3/4 C sugar
2 T vanilla
Corn flake crumbs to cover

Preparation
Cook noodles as directed, toss with butter to melt. Combine the rest of the ingredients except corn flake crumbs. Pour into a greased 9X13 pan, cover in corn flake crumbs. Add a few dabs of butter and bake for 1 hour at 350 degrees.

78. Dorothy's Noodle and Cheese Kugel
Submitted by Dorothy Sharlin

Ingredients
12 oz. thin or medium sized noodles
½ stick butter
3 eggs
1 C. sugar
2 t. vanilla
1 lb. cottage cheese
½ pt. sour cream

Preparation
Boil noodles in salt water for 9-10 minutes. Drain. Melt butter into noodles (in the same pot). Mix eggs and the other ingredients and add to noodles, mixing thoroughly. Pour mixture into a greased or nonstick sprayed 9x13 pan. Bake at 350° for one hour. Remove kugel from oven and sprinkle it with cinnamon and sugar. Put back into the oven until melted.

79. Luxel Kugel from Donna
Submitted by Donna Codell

Ingredients
½ lb. wide egg noodles
8 oz. cream cheese
1 stick butter
2 c. milk
4 eggs, beaten
¼ c. sugar
Salt
½-¾ c. raisins
2 c. cornflakes, crushed
1 t. cinnamon
Butter for top

Preparation
Cook noodles according to the package directions. Drain. Soften cheese and butter at room temperature. Heat milk, but do not boil. Add cheese and butter and mix well. Blend beaten eggs and noodles, milk mixture, sugar, salt and raisins. Mixture will be a little watery. Pour into a 9x13x2 pan. Sprinkle cornflakes on top. Mix sugar with cinnamon and sprinkle over cornflakes. Dot with butter. Bake at 375° for 45 minutes. Makes 10-12 servings.

80. Noodle Kugel from Ryan
Submitted by Ryan Aronoff, from family friend, Geri Greenberg

Ingredients
8 eggs, beaten
3 cups milk
16 ounces cooked and drained noodles
16 ounces cream cheese
½ lb. butter or margarine
1 cup sugar
2 T vanilla
Cornflake crumbs for topping
Cinnamon for topping

Sugar for topping

Preparation
Melt cream cheese and butter in microwave. Add milk and sugar and cook low in microwave, stirring often until dissolved. Mixture should be a light custard consistency. Remove from microwave. Add eggs and vanilla. Mix with cooked noodles and pour into a 9x13 greased pan. There will be some left over for another small pan. Put in refrigerator, preferably overnight. Before baking, sprinkle crumbs, cinnamon and sugar on top. Bake at 400 degrees for 15 minutes, then reduce heat to 375 degrees for 30 minutes or more if needed. Set the temperature 25 degrees less if using a glass pan.

**81. Recipe from Ronda Brooks currently residing in Commack, NY
Shared by her friend Paula Saltzman. It is from Paula's mother, Elaine Schneider**

Ingredients
1 package wide noodles cooked
1 stick melted unsweetened butter
8 oz. lite cottage cheese
8 oz. lite sour cream
20 oz. can of crushed pineapple in lite syrup- squeeze out most of the syrup
16 oz. can of peaches in lite syrup- remove syrup and slice up peaches
3 eggs
½ cup sugar
2 t. vanilla

Mix all of the above together and spread in a 9 x13 baking tray.

Topping
1 stick melted unsweetened butter
1 cup brown sugar
2 cups crushed corn flakes

Preparation
Combine all of the above and spread over the top of the noodle mixture. Bake uncovered at 350 degrees for about one hour. Uncover for the last few minutes to get a crispy topping.

82. Hope's Noodle Kugel
Submitted by Hope

Ingredients
16 oz. pkg. wide noodles
24 oz. cottage cheese
16 oz. sour cream
3 eggs, beaten
20 oz. can of crushed pineapple
3 c. crushed sugary cereal
3 T. sugar
3 t. cinnamon
¾ c. granulated brown sugar

Preparation
Beat and drain noodles. Beat eggs and sugar. Add cottage cheese and sour cream and mix well. Add drained, crushed pineapple. Add sugar and cinnamon. Mix together with drained noodles. Spray a 13x9 pan and pour mixture in. Top with the granulated brown sugar. Cover this with sugared cereal. Bake at 350° for one hour or until brown.

83. Bubi's Noodle Kugel
Submitted by Bunny Diamant
This is the recipe that her Bubi sent to her when she went away to college

Ingredients
1 package wide egg noodles
4 whole eggs
Salt and pepper to taste
2 Tbsp. vegetable oil

Preparation
Prepare noodles but cook for 2 minutes less than the cooking time on the package. Drain and set aside. Pour oil into baking pan and place in oven to heat. Beat eggs and add salt and pepper to taste. Mix with noodles. Coat bottom and sides of pan with hot oil. Pour extra oil from pan into noodles and mix gently. Pour noodles into pan and place in pan for 45-60 minutes or until golden brown on top. Cut and serve. It serves 6.

84. Sticky Bun Kugel
Submitted by Matthew Becker

Use your favorite noodle kugel recipe. Look up a recipe for sticky bun smear. And combine the two recipes. The smear goes on the bottom of the pan with walnuts and raisins. Place the noodle kugel on the top. Bake. When it comes out of the oven, flip the pan over. The syrup runs over the top like sticky buns.

85. Eileen's Noodle Kugel
Submitted by Eileen Schecter

<u>Ingredients</u>
1 lb. broad noodles
16 oz. cottage cheese
1 C. sugar
¼ lb. butter
16 oz. sour cream
2 eggs
⅓ c. golden raisins
a bit of cinnamon
A sprinkle of cornflake crumbs

<u>Preparation</u>
Cook noodles and drain as directed. Melt butter in the same pot that you cooked the noodles in. Use some butter to grease the casserole glass baking pan. Mix all of the ingredients together in the same pot and pour into the greased casserole baking pan. Sprinkle the top with cornflake crumbs. Bake one hour at 325 degrees. Let it sit before cutting.

86. Lemon Ricotta Kugel with Dried Fruit Medley
Submitted by Karen Levy

<u>Ingredients</u>
12 oz. pkg. wide egg noodles
8 oz. sour cream
15 oz. ricotta cheese
4 T. butter, melted

3 eggs, beaten
¾ c. sugar
Zest and juice from 2 lemons or ¼ c. of lemon juice
1 ½ t. Vanilla
Salt to taste
1 c. dried fruit medley
Cinnamon for topping

Preparation
Boil the noodles according to package directions. Drain and mix with melted butter. In another large bowl, mix together the remaining ingredients except for the dried fruit medley. Add the noodle mixture to the large bowl. Next, fold in the dried fruit. Pour everything into a greased 9x13 baking dish. Sprinkle the top with cinnamon. Bake at 375 degrees for 45-55 minutes until lightly brown.

87. Noodle Kugel from the Beth El Congregation
Recipe submitted by Arlene
Favorite from Beth Israel Congregation from Salisbury, Md.

Preheat oven to 350 degrees

Ingredients
1 lb. noodles
½ lb. butter
8 eggs, separated
1 cup sugar
½ tsp. salt
1 lb. cream cheese
1 pt. sour cream
1 tsp. vanilla

Preparation
Cook noodles. Mix butter, cream cheese and sugar together. Add egg yolks, salt, cottage cheese, sour cream and vanilla. Beat egg whites stiff. Combine other ingredients and mix well. Fold in the egg whites. Pour into a large, greased pan. Bake at 350 degrees for one hour.

Note: The synagogue usually makes a lot at one time. Can be baked for less time, frozen, and completely baking it at a later time. It is great reheated in the microwave.

88. Freddi's Kugel
Submitted by Freddi Seligman Givner of NYC
This kugel is made like a pancake

Mix boiled noodles with 3 eggs, salt and pepper. In a frying pan, put oil and a little butter. When hot, add the noodles, and cook until crispy. Flip and cook on the other side. When done, drain on paper towels. Cut like a pie.

89. Kugel from Carla's Great Grandma
Submitted by Carla Lorence living in Atlanta, Ga.

Ingredients
 1 (16 oz. pkg.) wide egg noodles
24 oz. cottage cheese
16 oz. sour cream
20 oz. can of crushed pineapple
2 c. crushed sugar cereal
3 T. sugar
3 t. cinnamon
¾ c. granulated brown sugar

Preparation
Boil and drain noodles. Beat eggs and sugar. Add sour cream and cottage cheese and mix well. Add drained crushed pineapple. Add sugar and cinnamon. Mix together with drained noodles. Spray a 13x9 glass baking dish. Add mixture to the pan. Top with granulated brown sugar. Cover top with crushed sugary cereal. Bake at 350° for one hour or until brown.

90. Grandma Goldie's Noodle Pudding
Submitted by Jeremy Shalom of New York

Ingredients
1 lb. (454 gm) package wide noodles, cooked and drained
6 eggs, beaten

1 16 oz. (475 ml) jar applesauce
1 cup (250 ml) white raisins
1 cup (250 ml) sugar
½ cup (125 ml) butter, melted
1 16 oz. (475 ml) can of crushed pineapple (juice discarded)
24-32 oz. ricotta cheese
1 tsp. vanilla extract
Cinnamon
Optional: add strawberries and/or walnuts

Preparation
Mix drained noodles with eggs, applesauce, raisins, butter, crushed pineapple and ricotta cheese. Add sugar, cinnamon and vanilla extract and mix well. Cover and bake at 350 degrees F (175 degrees C) for 1 hour. Uncover and bake 30 minutes longer. Makes 12-16 servings.

91. Lichen Kugel from Linda
Submitted by Linda Flack
This is her mother's recipe

Ingredients
1 lb. noodles
1 stick butter
8 oz. cottage cheese
2 T. sugar
2 1/2 cups milk
8 oz. cream cheese
8 oz. sour cream
6 eggs
Salt to taste
Cornflakes
Sprinkle of sugar and cinnamon

Preparation
Boil noodles in salted water until tender. Drain. Mix all of the ingredients together and place in a 13x9 greased baking pan. Crush cornflakes and sprinkle sugar and cinnamon on top of the

mixture. Bake at 350 degrees for one hour or until a knife inserted in the center comes out clean.

92. Dessert Kugel
Submitted by Evelyn Block

Ingredients
12 oz. cooked and well drained noodles
¾ c. cottage cheese
¾ lb. cream cheese
½ pt. sour cream
4 eggs
1 t. vanilla
½-1 t. salt
¾ c. sugar
1 c. milk
Graham cracker crumbs or fruit topping

Preparation
Mix all ingredients together except noodles. Add the noodles and mix well. Sprinkle top with ¼ c. stick butter butter and either graham cracker crumbs or fruit topping.

93. Cheesecake Kugel
Submitted by Maddie Zanuck Silverman

Ingredients
½ lb. fine noodles, cooked and drained
8 eggs
½ lb. butter or margarine
½ lb. cream cheese, softened
1 pt. sour cream
2 t. vanilla
1 c. sugar

For topping:
1 ¼ c. graham cracker crumbs

¼ c. sugar
⅓ c. melted margarine

Preparation
Spray 9x13 pan. Line pan with noodles. Blend together all of the ingredients and pour over noodles. Stir. Sprinkle top with graham cracker mixture. Bake one hour at 350°.

94. Nikki's Pineapple Noodle Kugel
Submitted by Nikki Hyames of London, England

Ingredients
1 tin pineapple in juice (chunks or slices)
Optional- small of pineapple slices to decorate
½ cup oil
¾ cup sugar
3 eggs
½ tsp vanilla sugar
250g noodles (8 oz)

Preparation
Cook noodles as per packet instructions. Drain and keep to one side 20x30 cm. (9.84 x11.81 in. pan). Mix the rest of the ingredients in one bowl (excluding the pineapple to decorate). When mixed, add to noodles and stir until evenly coated. Pour into oven proof dish. Decorate with pineapple slices. Cook in oven, uncovered, for 40 minutes at 180 degrees C (350degrees F).

Voila!

95. Gluten Free Noodle Kugel
Submitted by Sherrie Gilfor residing in Enfield, Ct.

Ingredients
½ lb. GF thin spaghetti or egg noodles (cut into small pieces)
1 pint sour cream
½ lb. butter
8 oz. cream cheese
2 t. vanilla

1 cup sugar
8 eggs

Preparation
Cook noodles as directed. Mix all of the ingredients (except noodles) together making sure to add eggs one at a time. Mix in noodles. Put everything into a 9x13 pan sprayed with no stick cooking spray. Sprinkle top with mixture of cinnamon and sugar. Bake at 350 degrees F for one hour.

Sherrie states that she usually uses low fat sour cream and cream cheese as well as fake sugar. This is a very adaptable recipe.

96. Aunt Florrie's Sweet Noodle Kugel
Submitted by Shelley Radbell from Queens, NY

Ingredients
1 lb. egg noodles
1 c. sugar
1 lb. cottage cheese
1 ½ t. Vanilla
1 c. golden or crimson raisins, dried apricots or prunes-chopped
7 eggs
3 c. milk
1 pt. sour cream
¼ lb. melted butter

Topping
⅓ c. crumbled corn flakes
1 t. cinnamon
1 t. sugar

Preparation
Cook noodles according to package directions. Mix all pudding ingredients together in a large bowl. Pour into a pan and refrigerate overnight, or for a minimum of 3 hours. Consistency will

be loose before refrigeration but will set when chilled. When ready to bake, mix topping ingredients in a small bowl and sprinkle over pudding. Dot with butter and bake for 350 degrees for 1 ½ hours until golden brown on top.

97. Valerie's Noodle Kugel
Submitted by Valerie Cohen

Ingredients
16 oz. package extra wide noodles (cook according to package directions al dente)
24 oz. small curd cottage cheese
1 c. sugar
5 large eggs
½ c. raisins
1 can pineapple chunks
1 stick butter (½ melted in 9x13 greased glass pan before mixture goes in and ½ melted in mixture)
¼ to ½ t. cinnamon

Preparation
Mix sugar and eggs in a large bowl. Add the rest of the ingredients, ending with the noodles. Gently stir with a very wide spoon. Pour into the pan. Sprinkle cinnamon on top. Bake at 350 degrees for 1 hour.

98. Debbie's Noodle Kugel
Submitted by Deborah Levine-Powell residing in Westchester County, NY

Ingredients
1 lb. broad egg noodles
5 eggs
½ c. sugar
1 lb. cottage or ricotta cheese
1 pt. sour cream
1 ½ t. vanilla
¼ c. melted butter
¾ c. golden raisins
1 t. cinnamon
1 can crushed pineapple (optional)
¼ c. brown sugar
cinnamon sugar for topping
Maraschino cherries for topping

Preparation
Cook noodles. Mix all of the ingredients together. Place in a buttered 13X9 inch pan. Top with the cinnamon sugar. Dot with butter and bake for 1 to 1 ½ hours at 300 degrees. Let cool and top with maraschino cherries.

Chapter 3: Vegetable and Fruit Kugels

1. Diane's Carrot Kugel
Submitted by Diane Goldring Jacobs from West Bloomfield Township, Mi.

Ingredients
½ c. brown sugar
¾ c. shortening
2 eggs
1 ½ c. grated carrot
1 scant c. flour
1 t. baking powder
½ t. salt
½ t. baking powder dissolved in 1 t. cold water
2 T. lemon juice
Optional: raisins that have been plumped in hot water

Preparation
Cream shortening and sugar. Add eggs and carrots. Slowly add flour mixture sifted with other dry ingredients. Add lemon juice plus soda mixture. Grease an 8x8 pan generously. Bake in a 375° oven for 30 minutes. Unmold after cooling for 15 minutes.

2. Laura's Apple Streusel Noodle Kugel
Submitted by Laura Ritter Maisto living in San Antonio, Tx.

Ingredients
Streusel Topping
(can be made in advance and frozen until needed)
¾ cup flour
¾ cup sugar
1 Tablespoon water
1 ½ Teaspoon cinnamon
¼ cup butter softened
Mix all ingredients in food processor until crumbly

Apple Kugel
1/3 cup sour cream
¼ lb cream cheese
1 lb whipped cottage cheese or ricotta cheese
4 eggs
½ cup whole milk
1 ½ cups sugar
2 Tsp vanilla
8 oz egg noodles
4-6 apples peeled and sliced very thin
2 Tablespoons sugar
1 Tsp cinnamon
Juice from ½ lemon

Preparation
Cook noodles and drain. Slice apples and add lemon juice to prevent browning. Mix apples with sugar and cinnamon and set aside. Mix all ingredients together EXCEPT APPLE MIXTURE. Pour noodle mixture into greased pan and add apple mixture in dollops throughout the noodles. Cover the entire mixture with Streusel topping. Bake for 1 hour at 350 degrees.

3. Zucchini and Mushroom Kugel
Submitted by Diane Dubey

Ingredients
4 zucchinis, quartered and sliced
1 pound of mushrooms, sliced
1 tsp salt
3 eggs
4 T potato starch
3 T onion soup mix
3 T olive oil
sugar is optional

Preparation
Sauté zucchini and mushrooms until cooked through. Transfer to strainer or colander and drain for at least 10 minutes. Combine with other ingredients and pour into a greased 9-inch round pan. Bake for an hour in a 350° oven.

4. Grandma Selma's Apple Kugel
Submitted by Jen Marzouk

Ingredients
1 pound of medium noodles
½ cup sugar
2 cups applesauce
½ pint low fat cottage cheese
2 tablespoons low fat sour cream
½ teaspoon salt
½ stick butter
4 eggs, beaten
1 cup golden raisins, optional
Cornflake crumbs

Preparation
Warm a 9x13 inch baking dish in the oven with butter. Brush butter around the pan. Pour off excess and save. Boil noodles in salted water for recommended cooking time. Drain. Mix noodles with all of the ingredients except butter and cornflake crumbs. Bake at 350° for about one hour and 15 minutes, until lightly browned.

5. Judith's Onion Kugel
Submitted by Judith Kierman Smith

Ingredients
4 large onions chopped
3 eggs
½ cup oil
½ cup water
¾ cup flour
2 tablespoon onion soup mix

1 tablespoon parve chicken soup mix
Salt & pepper to taste

<u>Preparation</u>
Mix all ingredients. Pour into an oiled (I use spray) 9x13 pan and bake at 350° for 55 minutes.

6. Beautiful Tri-Layered Vegetable Kugel
Submitted by Diane Dubey

<u>Ingredients</u>
Bowl 1
4 carrots
1 large, sweet potato
2 eggs
3-4 T potato starch|
2 T mayonnaise
1 tsp. salt
1 pinch pepper

Bowl 2
5 potatoes, peeled
2 eggs
3-4 T potato starch
2 T mayonnaise
1 tsp. salt
1 pinch pepper

Bowl 3
6 firm, large green zucchinis
1 large potato
2 eggs
3-4 T potato starch
2 T mayonnaise
1 tsp. salt
1 pinch pepper

Frying Pan
4 large onions, diced
3 T olive oil

Preparation
For each layer, boil the vegetables, drain and mash. Mix the vegetables in each bowl together. Keep them separated. Sauté the onions in olive oil until golden. Divide evenly among the three bowls. Take out a 10-inch round pie pan with removable sides, a springform pan, and coat it very lightly with some oil, very little. Pour the ingredients from Bowl 1 into the pie pan, and smooth it around. Pour the ingredients from Bowl 2 in next, and smooth it around. Pour the ingredients from Bowl 3 and smooth it down. Bake for 45-55 minutes, on 350, until firm and set.

When you are ready to serve, remove it from the baking pan. When sliced, the layers look beautiful.

7. Sweet Spaghetti Squash Kugel
Submitted by Meira E. Schneider-Atik from Queens, N.Y.

Ingredients
1 medium spaghetti squash
1/4 cup oil
3 eggs
Scant 1/2 cup sugar
Pinch salt
Cinnamon

Preparation
Using a sharp knife, cut a long gash in the squash lengthwise. Place in oven & roast at 350 for 20 minutes. Remove from oven. Using the gash as your guide, cut the squash in half. Remove seeds. Place squash halves cut side down on a tray & roast for 40 minutes. Remove from oven & turn squash halves cut side up to cool. When cool, scrape out flesh into a 9x13 baking pan. Add oil, eggs, sugar, salt, & a generous sprinkling of cinnamon. Mix well. Cover with foil & bake at 350 for 40 minutes.
Variation: if you want to add fruit such as crushed pineapple or grated apple, add fruit but reduce sugar to 1/4 cup.

8. Dorit's Squash Kugel
Submitted by Dorit Nieman

Ingredients
2 (10 ounce) packages frozen butternut squash thawed or 2 ½ cups peeled and cubed, or puréed squash
2 eggs beaten
½ cup flour or almond flour
½ cup light brown sugar, packed
½ teaspoon ground cinnamon
¼ teaspoon ground nutmeg

Preparation
Preheat oven to 350 degrees. Spray a 9-inch baking dish with non stick cooking spray. In a medium bowl place squash, eggs, flour and brown sugar: mix well. Pour mixture into prepared baking dish. Sprinkle with cinnamon and nutmeg. Drizzle with a little maple syrup if desired. Bake uncovered at 350 degrees F. For 30-40 minutes until set and edges are slightly golden. Serve warm or cold.

9. Carrot Ring Kugel
Submitted by Caroline Kalms from London, England

Cream 375 ml (375 g) margarine with 375 ml (1 ½ cups) brown sugar.
Add 6 whole eggs, 560 ml (2 1/4 cups) flour, 15 ml (3 tsp.) baking powder and 18 medium sized soft-cooked liquidized (made soft) mashed carrots.

Beat well and bake in greased bundt or chiffon tin for about 70 minutes, at 180°C (350°). Cool slightly and unmould. Fill with green peas in the center and serve hot. This can be made and reheated.

10. Squash Kugel from Shayna
Submitted by Shayna Philips Mauskop living in NY, NY.

Ingredients
Pie crust or graham cracker crust
1 box frozen squash

¼ cup sugar
¾ cup vanilla soy milk (parve)
4 egg whites
½ cup flour
1 drop vanilla extract

Preparation
Defrost squash by leaving it out at room temperature for a little while or microwave for a few minutes. Mix all of the ingredients together. Pour into the crust. Bake at 350 degrees for one hour or until firm.

11. Butternut Squash Kugel from Diane
Submitted by Diane Dubey living in Lincolnwood, Il.

Ingredients
2 (10-ounce) packages frozen butternut squash, thawed, or 2½ cups peeled and cubed, or pureed squash
2 eggs, beaten
½ cup flour or almond flour
½ cup light brown sugar
½ teaspoon ground cinnamon
¼ teaspoon ground nutmeg
maple syrup (optional)

Preparation
Preheat oven to 350°F. Spray a 9-inch round baking dish with non-stick cooking spray. In a medium bowl, place squash, eggs, flour, and brown sugar; mix well. Pour mixture into baking dish. Sprinkle with cinnamon and nutmeg. Drizzle with some maple syrup. Bake, uncovered, at 350°F for 30 to 40 minutes, or until set and edges are slightly golden.

12. Cabbage Kugel from our Ancestors
Submitted by Valerie Siegel

Chop cabbage and let stew in rendered fat until brown. The next day mix in the cabbage, ¼ c. loaf of bread, soaked in water and pressed dry. Add in 1/2c. brown sugar, ½ c. flour, ½ t. salt, ¼ lb. almonds,1 t. cinnamon, ½ c. diced oranges, 4 eggs, ½ lb. raisins, and the juice and peel of one lemon. In a large bowl, mix together all of the ingredients. Transfer to a well-greased pan. Bake at 350 F until done.

13. Laura's Mom's Kugel
Submitted by Laura Kahn

<u>Ingredients</u>
8 oz sour cream
12 oz apricot preserves
8 oz cottage cheese
1 tsp vanilla
2 eggs
¾ stick of butter

<u>Preparation</u>
Spray pan. Cut ¾ butter into slices. Boil noodles. Do not rinse. Place hot noodles into the pan. Add 2 eggs and mix. Add vanilla, apricots, sour cream and cottage cheese. Bake at 350 degrees for 45 minutes.

14. The Best Apple Kugel
Submitted by Sarah Bar-Ezer from Jerusalem, Israel

<u>Ingredients</u>
3 eggs
1 ½ c. sugar
Beat together
Add 1 c. oil and mix.
Add:
2 c. flour
¾ tsp baking soda
½ tsp salt

<u>Preparation</u>
Mix all ingredients together. Thinly slice 4-5 apples in a food processor (not granny smith, I like golden delicious, best) and mix into batter. Pour into 2 long English cake pans plus 1 short English cake pans or muffin tins (fill only halfway because they grow a lot). Mix 2 Tbsp sugar

with ¼ tsp cinnamon and sprinkle on top. Bake at 350°. For English cake pans bake 45-55 minutes depending on your oven and muffins bake for 25 minutes.

15. Spaghetti Squash Kugel
Submitted Diane Dubey

Ingredients
Small spaghetti squash cooked and shredded
1/2 cup spiralized zucchini.
Small onion and some mushrooms sautéed. You can use chives instead of onions.
1/4 cup oil
3 eggs
1/2 T salt and pepper

Preparation
Mix all of the ingredients together. Put a drop of oil in pan and put it in hot oven and add mixture to hot pan. Bake in a preheated 400-degree oven for 1 hour.

16. Ima Audrey's Squash Kugel
Submitted by Ima Audrey

Ingredients
6 or more baby squash (crookneck yellow are easy to peel)
Steam or boil 6 or more baby squashes strain and mash.
2 beaten eggs
1/4 and 1/2 potato starch
1/2 cup sugar
1 cup non-dairy creamer or non-dairy whip topping.
2 tsp vanilla or 2 tsp vanilla sugar.

Preparation
Mix all ingredients together. Pour into a greased baking pan. Sprinkle cinnamon on the top. Bake at 350 degrees for 30 minutes or until done.

17. Malky's Apple Kugel
Submitted by Mindy Rosengarten of Cedarhurst, N.Y.

Ingredients
5 Cortland or green apples, peeled and sliced
A handful of cut up strawberries
½ c. sugar
½ c. oil
¼ c. flour
1 egg
1 t. baking powder
1 t. vanilla
Some cinnamon

Preparation
Place the apples and strawberries in an 8x8 baking dish. Sprinkle with cinnamon and sugar. Mix the remaining ingredients and spread over the top. Bake in a preheated 350° for 1 hour.

18. Ilene's Vegetable Kugel
**Submitted by Ilene Darrish Ehrlich living in St. Louis, Mo.
This is a variation of her Mom's**

Ingredients
1 cup minced zucchini
1 cup minced onion
1 cup minced carrots
1 cup minced celery
1 cup minced mushrooms
6 schmaltz or oil
8 Matzos broken up- more if needed
10 1/2 oz can chicken broth (or half onion soup)
1 1/4 cup hot water
1 teas. salt
1/4 teas. pepper
2 teas. paprika
2 slightly beaten eggs

Preparation
You can add or subtract any vegetables that you like- the original recipe only had carrots, onions & celery. You will need a really big frying pan for this recipe as written. I use my food processor to mince the veggies. Heat oven to 375°. Sauté vegetables in schmaltz until tender. Add broken matzo and set aside. Mix soup and water together, add seasonings & eggs and combine with matzo mixture, adding more matzo if mixture is too liquid. Bake in a greased 13X9" pan for 30 minutes until slightly brown.

19. Apricot and Apple Streusel Kugel
Submitted by Diane Dubey

Ingredients
Apricot Layer
1/2 cup sugar
2 eggs
1/3 cup oil
1 package vanilla sugar
1 cup flour
1 teaspoon baking powder
1/4 teaspoon salt
10 fresh apricots, pitted and thinly sliced

Apple Layer
3 apples, peeled and thinly sliced
3 T sugar
1/2 teaspoon lemon juice
1/2 teaspoon cinnamon

Streusel
1/3 cup flour
1/4 cup brown sugar
1/8 cup sugar
1-1/2 tablespoons oil

Preparation
Preheat oven to 350 degrees Fahrenheit (180 degrees Celsius).

For the apricot layer, add sugar, eggs, and oil in mixer; beat together till light and fluffy. Add the rest of the ingredients, except for apricots, and mix well. Add apricots at the end, mixing just until coated. Pour into round shatterproof glass dish pan lined with baking paper. Level with a spatula and set aside.

For the apple layer, mix together all ingredients in a bowl and gently place on top of apricot layer, smoothing as you go along.

Mix together streusel ingredients in a small bowl. Sprinkle evenly over apple layer. Bake for 50–60 minutes or until fruit is soft and topping is crispy.

Note: When warming a frozen kugel, be sure to leave the kugel only partially covered for a few minutes and then uncovered for the rest of the time, so the topping doesn't get soggy.

Variation: For a healthier version, use whole wheat pastry flour, half oil and half applesauce in the apricot layer and just 1/3 cup sugar. Cut the oil in the topping to one tablespoon.

20. Rikki's Onion Kugel
Submitted by Rikki Eisner
Credit goes to Tsippy Nussbaum

Ingredients
6 onions-sliced
1 C. water
½ C. oil
5 eggs
½ C. potato starch
1 t. salt
½ t. pepper

Preparation
Layer onions in a sprayed 9x13 pan. Mix the rest of the ingredients and pour on top. Bake at 350 degrees for 1 hour.

21. Eggplant Kugel
Submitted by Gail Hochman

Ingredients
1 large eggplant
4 T. margarine
1 onion, chopped
1 green pepper
salt/pepper to taste
¾ c. crumbs
⅓ c, melted margarine
Paprika

Preparation
Onion and pepper can be mixed in food processor. Preheat oven to 350°. Peel eggplant and simmer in pot of covered water for 20 minutes. Drain. Mash. Meanwhile, sauté onion and pepper until tender but not crisp. Mix eggplant with slightly beaten eggs. Season with salt and pepper. Add onion and pepper. Blend in crumbs to hold-placed in a greased casserole. Put melted margarine on the kugel and sprinkle with paprika. Bake for 45 minutes.

22. Diane's Onion Kugel
Submitted by Diane Dubey

Ingredients
5 large onions, chopped
1/2 cup canola oil
4 eggs
3/4 cup water
1-1/2 cups flour
1 teaspoon baking powder
3 T onion soup mix
Black pepper to taste
1 can mushrooms, drained (optional)

Preparation
Preheat the oven to 400°F. Spray a 9x13 baking pan with non-stick cooking spray. Chop onions. Heat 1/4 cup oil in a large frying pan. Sauté onions until transparent. Set aside to cool.
In a large bowl, mix the rest of the oil with eggs and water. Add cooled sauteed onions. In a small bowl, mix flour with baking powder. Stir into the onion-egg mixture. Spice with onion soup mix and pepper. Add mushrooms, if desired. Spoon mixture into the greased pan.

Bake, uncovered, at 400°F for 45-60 minutes, or until golden brown on top.

23. Family Favorite Carrot Kugel
Submitted by Sheila Small
Passed down from her mom and has been a family favorite for years

Ingredients
1 lb. carrots
1 cup oil (or ¾ cup oil and ¼ cup water)
2 eggs
½ cup brown sugar
1 ¼ cups flour
1 tsp. salt
½ tsp. baking powder
½ tsp. baking soda
1 tsp. vanilla
1 tsp. lemon juice

Preparation
Cook and mash carrots. Combine with all other ingredients. Bake in a greased, 8 cup (2 quart) bundt pan at 359 degrees for one hour.

For a larger kugel, make recipe and a half, and bake in a 12 cup bundt (3 quart) bundt pan. Enjoy!

24. Broccoli Kugel from Fran
Submitted by Fran Kolin from NYC

Ingredients
4 boxes frozen, chopped broccoli, defrosted and drained
6 eggs
1 envelope onion soup mix,
4 large onions (fried ahead of time)
1 cup mayo

Preparation
Fry onions in oil until caramelized. It is best done the day before, or a few hours earlier than needed. Beat eggs with soup mix and mayo. Add the chopped broccoli, and then the fried onions. Spray a 9x13 pan with nonstick spray. Pour in mixture. Bake as is or sprinkle the top with some matzah meal during Passover or panko during the rest of the year.

25. Five Vegetable Kugel
Submitted by Marlene Abrams

Ingredients
5 eggs
1 lb. asparagus
3 zucchinis
3 medium yellow squash
1 c. spinach
½ c. carrots
½ t. basil
½ t. salt
3 T. butter or margarine, melted

Preparation
Combine all of the seasonings. Grate the asparagus, zucchini, yellow squash, spinach and carrots using a food processor. Drain and dry the vegetables. In a large bowl, beat the eggs. Add in the seasonings, vegetables, and butter or margarine. Bake for 40 minutes. Enjoy!

26. Walnut and Broccoli Kugel
Submitted by Stan Alpern

Ingredients
½ c. ground walnuts
1 large package of frozen broccoli, chopped
1 t. minced garlic
¾ c. mayonnaise
2 pkgs. onion soup mix
4 eggs
Shredded cheddar cheese for topping (optional)

Preparation
Mix all of the ingredients together in a bowl. Transfer to a 13x9 greased baking dish. Top with cheddar cheese. Bake at 350 degrees for one hour.

27. Nana Elma's Kugel
Submitted by Karen Pomerance. This recipe is from her Mum. Her children and grandchildren love it and they always talk about her when they eat it. Karen is from London and made Aliyah to Israel two years ago

Ingredients
1 packet frozen mixed broccoli and cauliflower
2-3 eggs
3-4 T. mayonnaise
Salt and pepper
Dried onions (optional)

Preparation
Boil the broccoli and cauliflower until soft. Drain. Mix eggs and stir them into the vegetables. Add the mayo, salt and pepper. Stir well, pour into dish, add dried onions. Bake 30-40 minutes. Enjoy.

28. Corn Kugel
Submitted by Diane Dubey

Ingredients
1/2 c margarine (melted and slightly cooled)
1/4 c sugar
4 eggs
1/2 c flour
1 tsp baking powder
3/4 tsp salt
3 cans of corn- 2 creamed and 1 regular, or 1 creamed and 2 regular corn.

Preparation
Mix margarine and sugar, add eggs, other ingredients and mix well. Bake on 375 covered for 1 hour. Uncover and cook for 15 to 20 minutes longer.

29. Onion Kugel
Submitted by Enid Briton from NY

This is my mother's recipe. The quantities are approximate. It is all about look and texture. Every time I make it is slightly different but always delish.

<u>Ingredients</u>
2 packages of wide curly noodles (whatever is on sale) COOKED
2-4 onions grated or food processed. Do not drain onion juice
8-12 eggs (this is the hardest part) when mixed into the noodles it should look slippery, not dry
1/4th-½ cup oil (not olive)
Salt to taste
A little pepper

<u>Preparation</u>
Use a large mixing bowl.
1. Cook noodles until al dente and drain. Let cool a bit before adding eggs.
2. Add eggs make sure its slippery and loose
3. Add grated onions
4. Add oil a little at a time. It should look shiny
5. Add salt and pepper
6. Mix everything together

You can make one large one or individual ones using a muffin tin. Whatever you use, grease it well and then heat it in the oven. This makes it easier to get out of the pan. Bake 350 F for 45 minutes until the top is brown and crunchy. This can be made ahead and frozen but then bake only until light brown on top and finish off when you want to use it.

Chapter 4: Potato, Rice, Bread and Vegan Kugels

1. Broccoli-Potato Kugel
Submitted by Diane Dubey

Ingredients
1 medium onion, diced
3 T vegetable oil, more for greasing the pan
3 cloves garlic, chopped
2 large potatoes (about 2 pounds), peeled and boiled
6 large eggs
1/3 cup mayonnaise
1/3 cup matzo meal
1 T salt
1/2 teaspoon ground pepper
2 pounds broccoli, cut into florets and cooked
4 T panko or challah crumbs.

Preparation
Sauté onion in 2 to 3 tablespoons oil in a small frying pan over medium heat until browned. Add garlic and stir for a minute or two. Set aside. In a large mixing bowl, mash potatoes and stir in eggs, one by one, incorporating well. Add mayonnaise, matzo meal, salt and pepper, stirring well. Fold in onion and broccoli. Grease a 9x13-inch baking pan and spoon in mixture, spreading evenly. Sprinkle with panko or challah crumbs. Preheat oven to 350 degrees and bake kugel for 50 minutes or until golden brown.

2. Bernice's Potato Kugel
Submitted by Allison Ivy
This recipe is from her Nana Bernice, from Queens, NY

Ingredients
2 potatoes
2 carrots
2 onions
2 zucchinis
5 eggs, beaten

3 c. matzo farfel
1 stick margarine, melted
Parsley (shredded a lot)

Preparation
Bake in a 9x13 pan at 350 degrees for 1 hour to 1 hour and 15 minutes.

3. An Easy Potato Kugel
Submitted by Diane Dubey

Ingredients
2 Spanish onions
6 potatoes
1 parsnip
1 zucchini
6 eggs
1½ T salt
½ teaspoon black pepper
1/3 cup oil

Preparation
Preheat oven to 350 degrees. Pour 1/3 cup oil in 9x13 baking pan. Place baking pan in the oven with oil. It is important for the oil to become hot. Meanwhile, grate onions, potatoes, parsnip and zucchini with a box grater or food processor. Add eggs, salt and pepper. Mix until incorporated. Take out pan with oil from oven and place potato mixture in pan. Bake for an hour or until kugel is brown and crunchy on the top.

4. Annie's Rice Kugel
Submitted by Susan Hoffman Klassman from Northeast Philadelphia

She told this sweet story. Her Mommom always made a rice pudding that was really a kugel.it was so good that as a kid she would eat it for every meal until it was gone! She never measured anything. Susan finally had to have her make it, so she could write it down.
Annie: Boil a pot of water. Add some rice. Put a lid on the pot and cook until done.
Susan: How much rice?
Annie: A glass.

Susan: A glass? What kind of glass?
Annie: A sour cream glass.
Susan: A big one or a small one?
Annie: A small one.
Susan: Okay, so that would be like a cup of rice. Now figure out how much water to boil for the brand of rice you're using.

Now for the rest of the recipe:
4 eggs, beaten
1 qt. milk
½- ¾ c. sweetener of your choice
½ c. or more of golden raisins

<u>Preparation</u>
Mix all of that together in a bowl. Add the cup of cooked rice. Pour into a greased 2-quart casserole dish. Dot with butter. Sprinkle with cinnamon.
Bake at 350° for 1 hour or until set and the sides are golden.

5. Challah Vegetable Kugel from Diane
Submitted by Diane Dubey

<u>Ingredients</u>
1/2 standard-size challah
1 large onion, diced
1–2 cloves of garlic chopped or 1-2 cubes of frozen garlic
1 stalk of celery
1 small green pepper
4 ounces of mushrooms, sliced
Salt and pepper to taste
Oil for sautéing
3 eggs

<u>Preparation</u>
Preheat the oven to 350 F. Soak challah in hot water for a few minutes. Transfer the challah to a strainer and squeeze out the excess water. Put the challah into a bowl. Heat the oil in a medium frying pan over a medium flame. Add the onion and sauté it with the garlic, celery, and green pepper until the vegetables are soft. Add the mushrooms towards the end and sauté just

a little more. Add the vegetables to the challah. Add salt and pepper and then the eggs, and mix well. Pour the mixture into a greased 9-inch-round pan. Bake for 45 minutes or so, until the top is brown and crispy. Cool before slicing.

6. Ima's Sweet Potato Kugel with Pineapple
Submitted by Ima Audrey

Ingredients
4 sweet potatoes
1-pound carrots
1 cup brown sugar
1 medium size can of crushed pineapple
2 eggs

Preparation
Peel and cut into small pieces, both carrots and sweet potato. Boil together. When they test soft, drain off into a colander and place the hot vegetables back into the pot. Mash with potato masher and add brown sugar, beaten eggs, and can of crushed pineapple. Mix well and bake in a 9"x13" pan. If you want it to be a little sweeter, sprinkle the top with brown sugar. Serve as a side dish to meat or chicken.

7. Potato and Leek Kugel
Submitted by Diane Dubey

Ingredients
9 medium russet potatoes (about 4 1/2 pounds), peeled
7 tablespoons vegetable oil, divided
3 medium leeks, white and pale-green parts only, thinly sliced crosswise
2 1/2 teaspoons salt
3/4 teaspoon freshly ground black pepper, divided
2 garlic cloves, finely chopped
1 small onion
4 large eggs, lightly beaten
1 tablespoon plus 1 teaspoon fresh thyme leaves, divide

Preparation

Preheat the oven to 375 degrees. Place 4 potatoes into 1" chunks and place in a medium pot. Cover with cold water by 1". Season water generously with salt, bring to a boil over medium-high heat, and cook until potatoes are tender, 10-12 minutes. Drain well, transfer to a large bowl, and mash with a potato masher; set aside.

Meanwhile, heat 2 Tbsp. oil in a large skillet over medium until simmering. Add leeks, 1/4 tsp. salt, and 1/4 tsp. pepper and cook, stirring frequently, until softened and golden, 5-8 minutes. Add garlic and cook until fragrant, 1-2 minutes more. Remove pan from heat and let cool slightly.

Grease bottom and sides of an 8x8" baking pan with 2 Tbsp. oil. Place pan in the oven for 10 minutes.

Meanwhile, grate 3 potatoes and onion using the large holes of a box grater or a food processor fit with a shredding blade. Wrap potatoes and onion in a clean dish towel or several layers of paper towels and squeeze out as much liquid as you can; add to the bowl with the mashed potatoes. Stir in sautéed leeks and garlic, eggs, 2 Tbsp. oil, 1 Tbsp. thyme, 2 tsp. salt, and 1/4 tsp. pepper; mix until well combined.

Thinly slice remaining 2 potatoes and toss with remaining 1 Tbsp. oil, 1 tsp. thyme, 1/4 tsp. salt, and 1/4 tsp. pepper in a medium bowl; set aside. Carefully remove preheated pan from oven and transfer potato-onion mixture to the pan (it should sizzle when it hits the hot oil). Smooth out the top. Layer potato slices over the top in a shingled fashion. Bake until golden brown and cooked through, 60-75 minutes. If you would like a crispy crust, place in broiler for 1-2 minutes.

8. Flour Kugel
Submitted by Mona Allen from Dallas, Texas
She said it is the easiest and quickest kugel ever and is always a hit.
This is the basic recipe, but she often mixes it with herbs and a mixture of onion and couchette (zucchini)

Ingredients
3 lg onions, diced
1 c flour

1 t. baking powder
1/2 c oil
3 eggs
1 T. chicken soup powder

<u>Preparation</u>
Preheat the oven to 400 degrees. Spray an 8x8 cooking pan (I usually use a loaf tin). Mix all the ingredients together and pour into the pan. Bake for about 45 mins.

9. Ruth's Vegan Sweet Potato Kugel
Submitted by Ruth Isaacs-Holzer living in South Bend, In.

<u>Ingredients</u>
8-10 sweet potatoes
4 T. margarine OR frozen olive oil
1/4 c. wine,
1/2 c. orange juice
3/4 t. salt
Topping
1-2 apples
lemon juice

<u>Preparation</u>
Bring peeled, sweet potatoes in a pot with water and cover to boil. Cook until soft. Drain and place in a bowl. Add the rest of the kugel ingredients to the warm potatoes. Warm all together. Spoon into 2 greased 8-inch pans. Peel apples. Cut into eighths. Slice thinly. Dip into lemon juice to prevent oxidation. Arrange in an attractive pattern on top of kugel. Bake in 350-degree oven for 30-40 minutes.

** Variation- In Step 2- for a sweeter kugel, add ½ c. sugar and 3-4 T. potato starch to the mixture (the sugar loosens the mixture. The starch thickens it again).

** In Step 3, layer sliced apples attractively on top of sweet potatoes. Sprinkle with cinnamon-sugar mixture.

10. Delicious Potato Kugel
Submitted by Charlene Johnson from her neighbor, Cecile Blate

Ingredients
2 cups raw potatoes (measure after draining)
2 eggs, beaten
1 onion, minced
½ c. flour
2 T. butter
½ t. baking powder
Salt and pepper to taste

Preparation
Sauté onion in butter until lightly browned. Set aside. Add eggs to the potatoes. Sift together. Sift flour, baking powder, salt and pepper and add to the potato mixture. Blend in the onions. Pour into a well-greased quart baking pan and bake in a preheated 350° oven for one hour. The edges will be crispy.

11. Challah Kugel! Yum
Submitted by Mona Allen living in Dallas, Texas

Ingredients
1 leftover medium-sized challah, torn into small pieces
4 eggs
2 (20 ounce) cans crushed pineapple, drained
1 teaspoon vanilla
½ cup oil
½ cup sugar
2 tablespoons margarine

Preparation
Preheat oven to 350 degrees. Mix together all ingredients except margarine and pour into a 9x13-inch pan. Break margarine into small pieces and dot top of kugel. Bake for 45 minutes to 1 hour. Good hot, at room temperature or even cold from the refrigerator!

12. Carole's Vegan Potato Kugel
Submitted by Carole Maye residing in Leicester, England

6 peeled and grated potatoes, 1x large pureed onion, salt, pepper. Put all ingredients in a large bowl and mix well. Add enough oil to achieve the right consistency. Pour into an oven proof dish and cook in a hot oven for about 40 mins (depending on size).

13. Ronda's Rice Kugel
Submitted by Ronda Dorfman currently residing in Warminister, Pa.

Ingredients
1 cup cooked rice
1 cup sour cream
5 eggs
1 lb. cottage cheese
¼ cup cream cheese
¼ lb. butter
⅔ c. sugar
1 c. milk
Corn flake crumbs

Preparation
Melt butter with corn flake crumbs. Spread on bottom of 9x9 pan. Mix together remaining ingredients. Pour on top of corn flake crumbs. Cook at 350 degrees for one hour and 15 minutes.

14. Fresh Hot Potato Kugel
Submitted by Diane Dubey

Ingredients
9 loose potatoes
9 eggs
1 cup oil
1 cup seltzer
Salt & black pepper

Preparation
Grate potatoes in food processor. Mix all ingredients together. Pour into a 9x13 pan. Broil on high for 20 minutes, uncovered, then bake at 400 degrees for 1 hour, uncovered.

15. Bread Kugel
Submitted by Rachel Furman Lewkowicz

Her mom loathed to throw food away, in particular bread. As she said, "it's a Jewish thing - we do not waste food, especially bread." So, her mom would save the ends and bits of pieces of bread that would get leftover from meals and freeze them. When she had a nice collection of this -- there would be all KINDS of breads -- she would remove the bread from the freezer and proceed to work magic and create BREAD KUGEL. This is one of Rachel's favorites and a great way to use up leftover bread bits.

Stuffing for the Kugel:
Ingredients
Leftover challot/bread – enough to fill a roasting pan to overflowing
1 large onion
3 medium carrots
4 thick stalks celery
1 TBS chicken, onion, or mushroom soup mix
¾ c olive oil
3 eggs, beaten
Salt, pepper, garlic powder, paprika – to taste

Preparation
Dice onion, carrots, celery finely. Toss with a little bit of olive oil, and the soup mix. Place in roasting pan, into 400° F oven, roast until veggies softened, just beginning to caramelize. Remove from oven.

Take challot/bread, tear into bite size pieces. Place in a colander and drain. Using hands, squeeze out excess water. Bread should be mushy. Add bread to cooked vegetables, mix well. Add olive oil and eggs and spices. Mix well. Spray the top with olive oil to give it a crispy top.

Bake at 400° F, until top is golden, slightly crispy, about 20–30 minutes.

16. Tasty Rice Kugel
Submitted by Charlene Johnson from her neighbor, Cecile Blate

Ingredients
1 c. rice
4T. butter
1 c. confectioner's sugar
3 eggs
¼ c. chopped nuts
½ c. raisins
½ t. cinnamon
Grated peel of 1 lemon

Preparation
Cook rice following package directions. Drain and set aside. Cream together the butter and sugar. Add cinnamon and lemon peel. Add eggs one at a time, beating after each one. Stir in the nuts and raisins. Add the rice to mixture. Bake in a well-greased 1 qt. baking dish for one hour at 350°.

17. Sharon's Vegan Potato Kugel
Submitted by Sharon Dobkin residing in Brooklyn N.Y.

Ingredients
1 bunch dill
¾ cups coconut oil
1 lb. baby carrots
2 potatoes
1 t. Himalayan salt
½ t. black pepper
1 t. dried parsley flakes
½ can coconut milk.
1 large onion
1 leek
2 stalks celery

Preparation
Chop up all of the vegetables. Heat the coconut oil and mix in dill. Add in the salt, pepper and parsley flakes. Add in the coconut milk, and all of the vegetables. Stir well. Pour into a pan lined with parchment paper. Bake at 350 degrees until browned.

18. Georgette's Family Potato Kugel
Submitted by Georgette Felco Roth, passed down through sight in her family

Ingredients
Left over mashed potatoes (the next day is better as they are less soft from being refrigerated)
1 small onion, grated
1 egg
Flour
Butter
Grated cheese

Preparation
Add one egg and grilled onion to your left-over mash potatoes. Make it into patties. Dust patties with flour. In an iron frying pan, melt butter and fry patties until golden brown on one side. Add some grated cheese and bake in oven for 5 minutes.

19. The BEST Potato Kugel Ever
Submitted by Rachel Furman Lewkowicz, from her mother, Helen Jacobs Furman
She grew up eating potato kugel made by my mom - Helen Jacobs Furman. She was introduced to the potato kugels served at kiddushim at shuls in the states. Rachel loved the texture of those potato kugels, but they were usually a bit too bland for her and wanted the flavor of her mother's kugel and the texture of the kiddushim kugels. And so, she began testing recipes -- with input from her mother, of course. Ultimately, after many experiments and tasting trials she came up with this one.

Bear in mind the following: It does not matter what kind of potatoes you use. Rachel has used red, white, yellow, large, small -- they ALL work. What is MOST important is the METHOD of preparation.

Ingredients

8 large potatoes (basically the foil baking tin in which you bake the kugel should be filled with potatoes)
2 large onions
1 ½ cup oil – any kind works
8 eggs (1 egg per large potato)
2 Tbs salt
1 tsp white pepper
1-2 Tbs lemon juice
Spray oil
3 – 4 cups water
1 tray of ice cubes

You will need:
Baking dish – I use the foil baking pans
2 Large mixing bowls
Whisk
Food processor or box grater
Wire mesh strainer

Preparation

Whisk all the eggs with 1 cup of the oil in a large mixing bowl. Set aside the rest of the oil for later. Put 3-4 cups of water in the second large mixing bowl. Add 1 – 2 Tbs of lemon juice and the ice cubes. Peel and cut into large chunks the potatoes and onions and put into the bowl of ice water. When all the potatoes and onions are peeled and cut you are now ready to grate. If using a food processor, use the coarse grating attachment. If using a box grater, use the coarse grating side. Grate as many chunks of potatoes and onions as can fit into the feeder of the food processor. Do a second group of grating. Empty the grated potatoes and onions into the wire mesh strainer (should be over or in your sink).

Using your hands, squeeze the grated mixture to remove as much of the water as possible. When there is little to no water left to squeeze out, put the grated mixture into the bowl with the beaten eggs and all. Mix well (I wear gloves and do much of the mixing using my hands).

Repeat steps 5 – 7 until all the potatoes and onions are grated. When using a food processor you will find that there will be some chunks or slices that do not get grated. Do not discard these! Remove the grater attachment from the food processor and replace it with the sharp rotary blade (like a blender blade). Put all the small leftover chunks into the food process and process on high. Add the processed potatoes to the potato, onion, egg and oil mixture. Mix well.

Add the salt, pepper, and reserved oil. Mix well. Pour mixture into baking pan. Spray top of mixture with spray oil – any kind. Bake in oven at 180 C until crusty golden brown on top.

Enjoy! (It tastes BEST when it first comes out of the oven so give yourself a treat and take a small piece for yourself then)!

20. Sweet Potato Kugel
Submitted by Stacey Williams

<u>Ingredients</u>
6 sweet potatoes, peeled and boiled
5 T. butter or margarine
3 eggs, beaten
½ c. sugar
3 t. baking powder
1 ½ t. salt

<u>Preparation</u>
Mash potatoes and add the rest of the ingredients. Mix well and place in a greased baking pan. Dot with margarine. Bake for 40 minutes at 350°.

21. Pan Fried Potato Kugel
Submitted by Phyllis Klughauot Becker of Ra'anana, Israel

This recipe is from her father's Tanta Lena made as latkes, and her Aunt Marcia turned it into a kugel. She had her NY cousin's kids come to visit her in Israel and she made their grandmothers' kugel for them. It made then feel right at home. She stated that across generations and miles and minor variations, it is always a family favorite. Phyllis said she has used an old simple blender, a food processor, or a hand grater to grate the ingredients.

Ingredients
In a medium sized frying pan:
Peel, wash, and chunk 4-6 potato
2-3 onions, grated
2 eggs
1 t. salt
a dash of pepper
2-3 T. oil

Preparation
Drain potatoes of the water. Heat oil to cover pan. Add the mixture. Fry until sizzle and brown on bottom. Cover with a flat metal (like the bottom of a spring form pan to carefully flip and slide onto pan to brown on the other side.

22. Daniel's Potato Kugel
Submitted by Daniel Marks of Maale Aduumin, Israel

He learned this from his mother, made a few twists of his own and was given an important tip by Dovid of Manchester fame.

Ingredients
2 eggs
3 T. flour
8 medium potatoes
1 very large onion or 2 medium onions
1 small beetroot
Baking powder
Salt and pepper to taste
4T. oil

Preparation
Dice and sauté half the onions and grate the other half. Peel and grate the potatoes and squeeze out the water. Peel and grate the beetroot. Mix the potatoes and beetroot and then add the onions and all other ingredients. Put in a 180 C. / 350 F. degree oven for about an hour.

This freezes very well indeed.

23. Marlene's Vegan Noodle Kugel
Submitted by Marlene Zider of Grayslake, Il.

No one in my family made sweet kugels, only savory. But, in order to make traditions for my grandchildren, I decided to "pass on" a sweet noodle kugel recipe. Since 3 of my grandchildren are vegan, as are their parents and I, I worked on converting a traditional recipe into an egg- and dairy-free vegan recipe. I make this with whole wheat pasta of any shape, but the recipe will work well with pretty much any type (but not egg!) and shaped pasta, even the flat noodles traditionally used! This recipe serves 4-16, depending on if it's being used as a main or side dish. Because of the tofu and pasta, this makes a very satisfying main dish—maybe even for breakfast!

Ingredients
8 oz (1/2 1-lb. box) pasta, cooked per carton instructions
7 – 8 oz tofu (1/2 of a 14-16 oz package), cut into cubes and drained
1 cup vegan cream cheese
¼ cup real maple syrup
1 tsp vanilla
½ cup unsweetened applesauce
½ cup raisins
4 Tbl unsalted vegan butter (ex: Miyoko's)
Ground cinnamon to sprinkle on top (optional: to personal taste—I use a dash)
Brown sugar to sprinkle on top (optional: to personal taste—I use 2 Tbl)

Preparation
Preheat oven to 350 degrees F; oil or spray a square 2-quart casserole dish. Put tofu in mixing bowl and mash with a potato masher until very well crumbled (you don't want bigger pieces that could taste like tofu). Add vegan cream cheese, maple syrup and vanilla; stir well. Stir in the pasta, applesauce, raisins and melted vegan butter, then transfer to greased casserole. If using, sprinkle on brown sugar and cinnamon. Bake for 40 minutes (if used, the brown sugar will caramelize on top). Let stand 10 minutes before cutting or pieces will fall apart.

24. Leya's Potato Kugel
Recipe submitted by Leya Meisels currently residing in Tzfat, Israel.

Ingredients
6 potatoes
1 small onion
½ cup oil
salt and pepper to taste

Preparation
Sauté onion in oil. Grate and blend potatoes together with onions. Add salt and pepper to taste. Put in an English loaf sized pan (8 ½ 4 ½ x2 ½). Broil on high for about 15 minutes until it has crust. Take out and put in a 400-degree oven for 1 hour and 15 minutes.

25. Vegan Sweet Potato Kugel
Submitted by Bev Graff, living in Plano, Texas

Ingredients
8-10 sweet potatoes
4 T. marg. or frozen olive oil
1/4th cup wine
½ cup orange juice
3/4th t. Salt

For topping
1-2 apples
Lemon juice
Cinnamon and sugar

Preparation
Bring peeled sweet potatoes in a pot with water to boil and cover. Cook until soft. Drain and place in a bowl. Add the rest of the kugel ingredients to the warm potatoes. Warm all together. Spoon into 2 greased 8-inch pans. Peel apples. Cut into eighths. Slice thinly. Dip into lemon juice to prevent oxidation. Arrange the apples in an attractive pattern on top of kugel. Bake in a 350-degree oven for 30-40 minutes Sprinkle with cinnamon and sugar mixture.

Chapter 5: Passover Kugels

1. Apple Matza Kugel
Submitted by Andrew Steinberg

Ingredients
4 large tart apples, cored
6 pieces matza
½ c. brown sugar
¼ orange juice
8 eggs
1 ½ c. sugar
½ c. butter or margarine, melted
1 c. golden raisins
1 c. dried apricots, chopped
1 t. salt
1 t. cinnamon
4 T. butter/margarine for topping

Preparation
Toss the apples with brown sugar and orange juice. Set aside. Break the matza into pieces and soak in warm water until soft. Beat eggs. Add sugar, salt, cinnamon, melted butter, raisins and apricots. Drain the water from the matza and add the matza to the egg mixture and the apple mixture. Blend it all well and pour into a lightly greased 10x14 pan. Dot the top with butter. Bake in a preheated 350° oven for 1 hour.

2. Anita's Passover Potato Kugel
Submitted by Jen Marzouk

Ingredients
5 lbs. potatoes, grated
7 small to medium onions, sliced thin
12 heaping tsp. of cake meal
5 t. salt- no more
10 eggs
4 t. sugar

2 ½ t. baking soda
2 T. oil

Preparation
Toss it all together and bake for one hour at 350°.

3. Passover Apple Kugel
Submitted by my daughter, Heather Jacobsohn, currently residing in Potomac, Md.

Ingredients
Ingredients for filling
3 apples, peeled and thinly sliced
1 t. lemon juice
2 T. sugar

Ingredients for crumbs
1 package of crushed ladyfingers
½ cup ground almonds
1 cup sugar
1 t. baking powder, optional but recommended
1 egg
½ cup oil

Preparation
Preheat oven to 350. Lightly grease a 9x13 baking pan.

To prepare filling: Place thinly sliced apples in a bowl, toss with lemon juice immediately to prevent browning. Add sugar and set aside.

To prepare crumbs: Mix together the ladyfinger crumbs, ground almonds, sugar and baking powder in a large bowl. Add the egg and oil and stir with your fingers until coarse crumbs are formed.

Place a little less than half of the crumbs on the bottom of the prepared baking pan. Spread the apple filling evenly over the crumbs. Pour remaining crumbs over the apples, spread in an even layer to ensure that all apples are covered.

Bake at 350 for about 40 minutes, until golden brown on top.

Note from Heather: The kugel was very thin when made as directed above. Next time she will make it (and there definitely will be a next time) she will bake it in a 10-inch round pan to make a slightly higher kugel.

Enjoy!

4. Myrna's Matzo Farfel Kugel
Submitted by Myrna Bachiochi currently residing Brentwood, Ca.

Use a mixture of chopped celery, onions and carrots. Sauté the vegetables until translucent. Put the matzo farfel in a colander and dampen it. Put it in a bowl and salt, pepper and a beaten egg. If it seems dry, add some chicken broth. Combine with the vegetables and put it into a greased baking pan. Bake until brown on top for about 45 minutes.
Es gesunte haid.

5. Spinach and Broccoli Kugel
Submitted by Susan Bryant

<u>Ingredients</u>
4 Matzahs, crumbled
2 cups water
3 T. oil
4 eggs
1 onion, diced
1 ½ cups frozen spinach
2 cups frozen broccoli
1 t. onion powder
½ t. garlic powder
½ t. pepper

Preparation
Put matzahs and water in a bowl and keep until all of the water is absorbed and the matzahs are mushy. Sauté onion and add to the matzah. Add defrosted spinach, oil, eggs and seasoning. Mix together.

Using a 7x11 inch pan, lined, place the frozen broccoli pieces at the bottom of the pan. Pour the matza mixing on top. Cover the pan on top with foil. Bake for one hour at 350 degrees. Uncover the pan and bake for a half hour more.

6. Ilene's Sweet Kugel
Submitted by Ilene Darrish Ehrlich of St. Louis, Mo.
This sweet kugel is a variation of her Aunt Lorayne's
Makes a small Kugel but can be doubled, tripled or whatever you need for the size kugel you want. My aunt's recipe only had apples and raisins. You can add or subtract any dried fruit of your choice. It uses matzo FARFEL, not mazo - it makes it very tender.

Ingredients
2 cups matzo farfel
2 eggs
1/2 teas salt
1/3 cup sugar
1 large apple- peeled, cored & sliced
1/2 cup dried fruit- any combination of raisins, quartered apricots or craisins
1 Tbls lemon juice
Cinnamon sugar to taste
3 Tbls oil

Preparation
Heat oven to 350°. Do NOT mix ingredients ahead of time, it gets too soft. It can be mixed in the casserole you will be using to bake it. Soak the Farfel in cold water and squeeze out the excess. Beat eggs and add along with the rest of the ingredients except for the cinnamon sugar and oil. Put in a casserole dish and sprinkle with the cinnamon sugar. Sprinkle the oil over the top. Bake for 30-40 minutes or until brown.

7. Mom's Matzo Kugel
Submitted by Amy Lambert from St. Louis, Missouri
Her Mom used to make it for her family, and Amy has carried on the tradition

Ingredients
Soak 4 sheets of matzo in water. Drain and mash.
4 eggs
¼ cup of sugar
½ cup of golden raisins
1 small can of crushed pineapple, drained
1 stick margarine, melted
1 teaspoon cinnamon
2 apples, peeled and sliced very thin

Preparation
Mix all ingredients well. Put into nonstick sprayed 8-inch square pan. Bake at 325 degrees for 1 hour.

To double recipe use a 9 x13 pan. Can make ahead and freeze. Reheats well.
Let cool a little while after baking so it can be cut into squares

8. Passover Pineapple Kugel
Submitted by Talia Sobol

Ingredients
4 eggs
½ C. oil
½ C. sugar
4T. potato starch
1 t. vanilla
1 t. baking powder
20 oz. can of crushed pineapple, drained
whole cored pineapple rings for topping

Preparation
Preheat oven to 350 degrees. Combine eggs, oil, sugar, potato starch, vanilla and baking pineapple rings. Bake for 40minutes or until golden brown. Powder. Add the crushed pineapple. Place in a round 9 in. baking pan. Top with cored pineapple rings. Bake for 40 minutes or until golden brown.

9. Renana's Passover Vegetable Kugel
Submitted by Renana's Kitchen Blog with permission
Renana lives in Israel.

Ingredients
5 eggs
1 sweet potato
2 carrots
2 zucchinis'
1 potato
3 matzos
4 tablespoons olive oil
Salt and pepper by your taste

Preparation
Heat the oven to 180° C/350°F with the fan. In a bowl, grate all vegetables. Wet the matzos under tap water for 30 seconds. With your hands, break the matzohs to small pieces and add to the vegetables. Add the eggs, olive oil, salt, and pepper. Mix well to a unified batter. Pour to a baking pan (9x13). Bake for 45 minutes. Cool at room temperature.

Have a piece and Happy Passover!

10. Ima Audrey's Mushroom Pesach Kugel
Submitted by Ima Audrey
She states that she usually doubles the ingredients as the Kugel comes out tasty, but very small.

Ingredients
2 lbs mushrooms... sliced
2 large onions... sliced
3 tbsp oil

3 eggs beaten
1/2 cup mayonnaise
2 tbsp potato starch
2 tbsp onion soup mix
Garlic powder to taste
Pepper to taste.

Preparation
Preheat oven to 350 degrees. Sauté onions in a pan with oil until they are soft, add the mushrooms and sauté another few minutes. Mix the rest of the ingredients together and add the mushroom mixture. Pour into a round pan and bake for about 45 minutes.

11. Pesach Carrot Kugel
Submitted by Ima Audrey

Ingredients
1 can of carrots or one pound cooked and mashed carrots.
2 T melted margarine
1/3 cup sugar
3 eggs
2 T potato starch
1 T vanilla extract
1 tsp vanilla sugar
1 T baking powder
Dash of cinnamon

Mash carrots very well.
Mix all of the ingredients together and then mix with the carrots.
Put in a greased pan.
Mix all of the ingredients together.

Topping
1/4 cup chopped walnuts
2 T sugar
2 T melted margarine
Mix together and spoon over carrot mixture.

Bake at 350 degrees for about 45 minutes or until done.

12. Apple Farfel Kugel
Submitted by Char Wolnik

Ingredients
3 c. matzo farfel
Hot water (to cover farfel)
5 eggs, separated
1 t. salt
¼ to ½ c. sugar
½ lb. margarine, melted
¾ to 1 c. crushed pineapple
2 c. applesauce
1 t. cinnamon
1 t. cinnamon sugar

Preparation
Place farfel in colander. Pour hot water over it. Beat egg yolks, salt, sugar and margarine. Mix with farfel. Add pineapple, applesauce and cinnamon. In a separate bowl, beat egg whites until stiff. Fold into above mixture. Spoon into round casserole. Sprinkle with cinnamon sugar. Bake at 350° for 35-45 minutes. Serves 8 people.

13. Ima's Pesach Banana Kugel
Submitted by Ima Audrey

Ingredients
2 cups farfel or 2 cups crushed matzah
1 cup cold water
2 eggs, beaten
1/4 cup sugar
1/2 tsp salt
2 T oil
1 cup sliced bananas
1/2 cup walnuts or chopped almonds (optional)

Cinnamon

Preparation
Moisten farfel or matzah with water and drain. Combine matzah with eggs, salt, sugar, oil, bananas, nuts and cinnamon. Mix and pour into a greased baking dish. Bake at 350° for 35 minutes.

14. Matzo Kugel from Ryann
Submitted by Ryann Ge-Jo
The secret of this kugel is that all of the apples are baked into it.
Serve it as a side dish or desert.

Ingredients
4 square matzohs
Water
7 eggs
¾ cups sugar
juice of ½ lemon
⅓ cup margarine
1 ½ teaspoons cinnamon
Salt to taste (optional)
4 large apples
½ cup raisins
¼ teaspoon salt
Grease for the pan

Preparation
Soak the matzos in a large bowl with water to cover. Drain and press out the excess water. Separate the eggs into two large bowls. Beat the egg yolks with sugar until light and fluffy. Add the drained matzos, lemon juice, margarine, cinnamon and salt. Beat until well combined.

Peel the apples and grate them into the egg mixture, add the raisins and mix to blend. With an electric mixer at low speed, beat the egg white with ¼ teaspoon salt until frothy. Increase to a high speed and beat until stiff peaks form. Gently fold the stiffly beaten egg whites into the yolk mixture. Lightly grease a 9 ¾ x13 ¾ inch baking pan. Turn the mixture into the pan. Bake in a preheated 375-degree oven for 30-45 minutes, until nicely browned. Serves 12-14.

15. Linda's Matzoh Kugel
Submitted by Linda Brenner currently residing in Vernon Hills, Il.

Ingredients
5 matzohs
3 eggs
½ t. salt
½ c. sugar
1 stick of melted margarine
1 t. cinnamon
½ t. light raisins
3 large Fuji Apples

Preparation
Break matzohs and soak in water. Beat eggs and add cinnamon, salt, sugar and raisins. Stir in apples and margarine. Heat for 50 minutes in a shallow dish at 350°.

16. Melanie's Zucchini and Potato Kugel
Submitted by Melanie Berenblut

Ingredients
3 courgettes (zucchini)
2 sweet potatoes
4 potatoes
Onion powder (add as much as you like depending on personal taste)
Matza meal
1 or 2 eggs, depending on size
Small amount of oil

Preparation
Peel potatoes and sweet potatoes. Grate them and mix together. Grate courgettes, add onion powder, a little matza meal, eggs and oil. Mix everything together. Grease 2 foil containers with oil. Bake at 350° for 50 minutes.

17. Aunt Helen's Matzoh Kugel
Submitted by Ryan Aronoff. This recipe is from his Great Aunt Helen Lubin
Prep time: 15 mins.
Cook time: 45 mins.
Difficulty: Easy
Servings: 12

Ingredients
8 matzohs
6 eggs
½ t. salt
1 t. cinnamon
1 cup raisins or craisins
4 large Red Delicious apples, pared and grated, or 1 cup applesauce
1 cup sugar
9 tbsp oil or ½ stick melted butter

Preparation
Break matzohs into pieces and place in colander. Run water over the pieces quickly and drain, don't press.

Grease 9 x13 pan. Beat eggs, adding salt, sugar and cinnamon. Add matzoh, then oil, raisins or craisins & apples. Bake for 45 minutes at 350 degrees.

When cool, cover and freeze.

18. Zucchini Kugel
Submitted by Sherry Weinstein

Ingredients
1 large zucchini
¼ c. oil
1 egg
1 c. matza meal

Preparation
Peel and grate zucchini. Add the rest of the ingredients. Bake in a preheated 350 degree oven for 45 minutes.

19. Matzo and Mushroom Kugel
Submitted by Lisa Eichler

Take at least one box of matzo, dampen and break into tiny, tiny pieces. Take one lb. of mushrooms and cut thick. Chop one onion. Mix together, add garlic, and stir fry it in a pan using olive oil and butter. You can add some spinach and cheese as well. Move to a greased 9x13 glass baking dish. Add 3 eggs, some spinach and cheese and blend everything. Bake until the top is golden brown, for about 30 minutes in a 350-degree oven. This can also be baked in a microwave for a few minutes instead.

20. Joan's Passover Pineapple Kugel
Submitted by Joan Sinclair

Ingredients
4 c. matza farfel
20 ounce can of crushed pineapple with juice
6 eggs
2 sticks of margarine, melted
1 ½ c. sugar

Preparation
Preheat oven to 325 degrees. Pour hot water over farfel and squeeze out the water. Beat the eggs and mix them together with all of the other ingredients. Bake in a greased 9x13 pan for 45 minutes.

21. Mini Meat and Matza Kugel
Submitted by Marie Beeler Howell from South Florida.

Ingredients
1 large, sweet onion, chopped
2 T. olive oil
1 lb. ground beef
1 T. minced garlic
16 oz. tomato sauce
½ t. salt
½ t. pepper
2 T. paprika
2 T. oregano
½ box of matzah, crushed
½ c. chicken broth
8 eggs, mixed well
¼ c. potato starch
1 c. chicken broth, boiling
2 mini muffin tins, 24 count each, brushed with vegetable oil

Preparation
sauté onion in the olive oil, add ground beef and garlic and cook until done. Add tomato sauce, salt, pepper, paprika and oregano. Cook for 10 to 20 minutes, until most of the liquid is absorbed. Add crushed matzah and mix well. Pour ½ cup of the chicken broth over to make sure the matzah is moistened. Cool completely. Mix in eggs. Sprinkle potato starch over mixture, pour boiling chicken broth over and stir well. Add a teaspoon of mixture into each muffin tin. You can also use a small cookie scoop. Bake at 350 degrees until puffed and crispy, about 20 minutes. Switch pans halfway through. Serve warm.

22. Passover Vegetable Kugel
Submitted by Shauna Lore who was born and raised in Vancouver, Canada and moved to Sydney, Australia over 24 years ago

This recipe is from her Mom, Phyllis Weinstein. Shauna said that her Mom expressed her love for people through her cooking and baking.

Ingredients
2 cups matza farfel, toasted very light
2 medium onions or leeks, diced
2 stalks celery, diced
2 medium carrots, grated fine
½ green pepper, diced
1 tbsp. chopped parsley
2 medium potatoes, grated and well drained
5 eggs, well beaten
½ cup oil
2 cups cold water
1 ½ tsp. Salt
1 ½ tsp. Pepper

Preparation
Soak farfel in water for 10-15 minutes. Pour off excess water; do not press. Sauté onions in oil; add celery, pepper and carrots; sauté until tender. Combine remaining ingredients. Pour into a hot, oiled 9x12 ovenproof dish. Bake for 35-40 minutes at 350 degrees (this tastes even better the next day).

Passover 1967

Kim, Grandma Bella, Brother Roy, and Dad Walter

Passover 1967

Kim, Mom Harriet, Sister Sue, Papa Benny, and Roy

Young Cousins

Pam, Nan, Roy, Sue, Kim, and Brenda

Kim

Toronto Family

Cousins Eddie and Annie, Walter, Tanta Frieda, Harriet, Heather, and Kim

Roy and Kim

Walter, Harriet, Kim, Nieces Jennifer and Heather

Jennifer, Roy, Kim, and Heather

Kim With Her High School BFF's

Jana, Sandy, Elaine, and Kim

Kim, Maria, Lorri, Cris, Grace, and Baby Jack

Kim

Family Thanksgiving 1987

Artie, Kim, Barbara, Roy, Barry, Pam, David, Bonnie, Steven, Larry, Walter, Loretta, and Brenda

Bris of nephew Benjamin & Baby Naming of niece Myriah

Roy, Paul, Myriah, Nan, Kim, Walter, Harriet, Benjamin, Jennifer, and Heather

Kim, Heather, Myriah, Jennifer, and Benjamin

Kim and Husband Dave

Kim and Her Joy of Cooking

Dad's 75th Birthday

Benjamin, Myriah, Nan, Kim, Heather, and Walter

Kim's Bridal Shower

Kim

Beach Wedding

Dave and Kim

Wedding

Kim

Aunt Emma, Lena, Walter, Nan, Cousin Rena, Jennifer, Myriah, Heather, and Kim

Dave and Kim

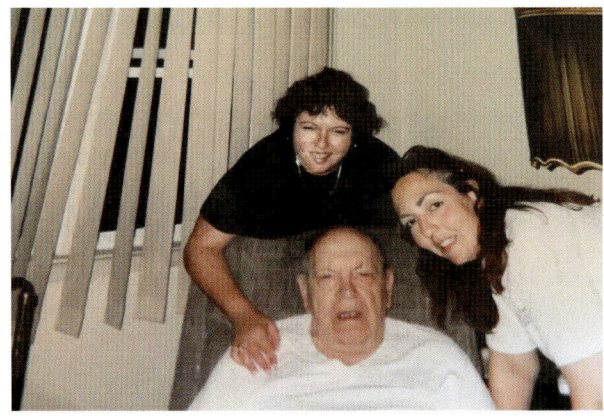

Nan, Kim, and Walter

Kim Playing Her Djembe Drum

Kim feeding her newborn son, Hudson on the date of his birth, December 15th, 2006

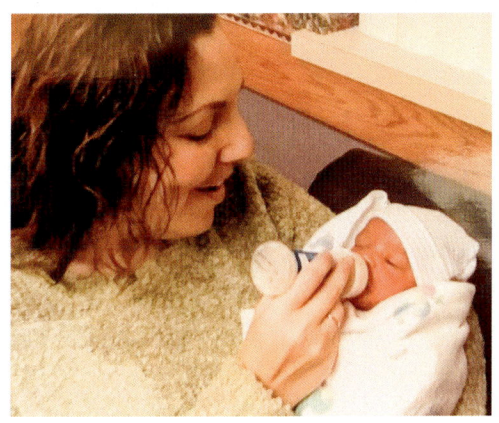

Kim and Hudson

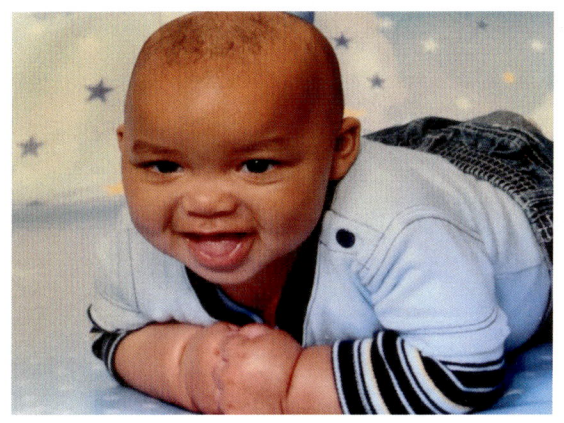

Hudson

Hudson

Party After Husdon's Bris

Dave, Kim, and Hudson

Roy, Walter, and Hudson

Rena, Walter, Nan, and Hudson

Rosh Hashanah 2007

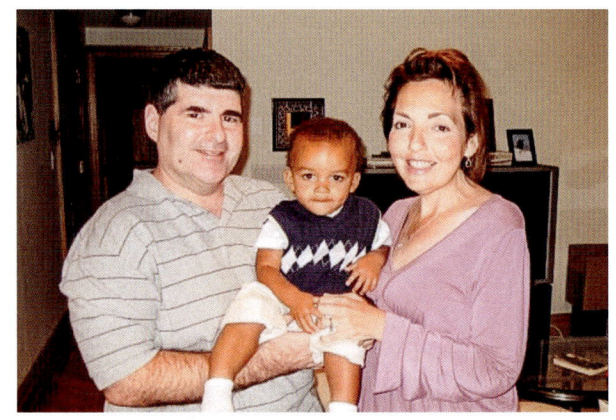

Dave, Hudson, and Kim

Hudson and a snake

Kim's great nephew and great niece

Dave, Gavin, Hudson, and Lilah

Roy and Hudson

Two more of Kim's great nephews

Hudson, Ethan, and Davis

Hudson

The Jacobsohns

Niece Heather, Avi, Shoshi, and Michael

The Chemijs

Davis, Niece Jennifer, Ethan, and Morgan

The Landesmans

Molly, Nephew Benjamin, Daisy and Luna

The Monicals

Gavin, Niece Myriah, Nick, and Lilah

Hudson

Hudson and Dave

Acknowledgements

This cookbook is the brainchild of many joyful conversations between my sister Kim and I. It is the inspiration for this book.

I owe an enormous debt of gratitude to everyone who has contributed their treasured recipes to this book. These kugel recipes come from the kitchens of people around the world.

To my friends, thank you for always being there for me. Through good times and bad times, I knew you were always there for me.

To Dawn Levy and Gal Cohen I am grateful for all of your assistance with my photographs. To Mallory Rose, for organizing, proofing and formatting, I owe you an enormous debt of gratitude.

Finally, to my family who have always supported me; both my immediate family and family members near and far, who have been a part of my life. You are my rock, my love, my heart. A special shout out to my nephew Hudson (who calls me Tanta Nan). Yor mother left a legacy, not of physical wealth, but what is really most important in life. She had strong convictions of justice and fairness, a strong sense of values, a love of cooking, laughter and music, and above all a love for her friends and family. We are all here for you to love you, support you, and cheer you on, every step of the way.